Counseling in Residence Halls

BY

RHODA ORME, Ed.D.

BUREAU OF PUBLICATIONS
TEACHERS COLLEGE, COLUMBIA UNIVERSITY
· NEW YORK, 1950 ·

Preface

THE preliminary bibliographical work and assembling of data for this project were begun during the year 1945–1946 when I was acting as dormitory counselor at Barnard College after a number of years' experience as instructor and academic dean at Bradford Junior College. My interest in counseling and the lack of information on the counseling aspects of the residence hall program made this a logical choice of project. This book, written in non-technical language and taking a middle-of-the-road position in the current controversy between directive and non-directive counseling, is addressed to inexperienced counselors and to those with some training and experience. It describes opportunities for counseling in dormitories and gives a brief treatment of the knowledge and skills needed. Concrete examples of counseling are used to clarify the text and to keep the focus on the dormitory setting for counseling.

My sources of data include (1) a survey of the literature on counseling and on dormitory work; (2) a questionnaire filled out by twenty colleges and universities, giving concrete examples of dormitory counseling, types of problems found, and sources for referral; (3) questionnaires filled out by, and interviews with, dormitory students, yielding data regarding student reactions to counseling and their need for counseling; and (4) recorded interviews and other contacts with dormitory students.

Since the dormitory affords an ideal setting and a variety of opportunities for counseling, I believe that this study has relevance. While it does not purport to be a textbook on the techniques of counseling, it is my hope that it will prove suggestive of method and be of some practical value.

I wish to thank Professors Beulah Van Wagenen and Clarence Linton, of Teachers College, Columbia University, for their helpful suggestions regarding the manuscript. My gratitude is also due to the heads of residence who filled out the questionnaire sent to the colleges and to the dormitory students who cooperated in questionnaires and interviews and to all other students who expressed their opinions frankly and thoughtfully. It is to Professor Ruth Strang that I am most deeply indebted for her detailed constructive criticism at all stages of the project. Without her encouragement and help it could never have been completed.

R.O.

Contents

Counseling
in
Residence Halls

Chapter One

INTRODUCTION

Two educational developments point to the need for a book on counseling in residence halls. One is the increase in counseling services on college campuses. The other is the growing recognition of the contributions of the dormitory program to personal development and to competence in social relationships. No longer are heads of dormitories thought of merely as social hostesses or as guardians of the physical and moral welfare of their students; they are now seen to be "friendly and resourceful counselors" (33:9),[1] with professional status.

PRESENT NEED FOR COUNSELING

The numerous articles and books on counseling which have appeared within the last few years are an indication of increasing interest in its potentialities. No educators and few laymen, even those extremists who advocate a "sink or swim" policy in dealing with students, would dispute the need for some form of counseling in college. College educators, in general, show an awareness of the values which effective counseling has, not only, or even chiefly, for the poorly adjusted but for all students. College personnel workers clearly recognize both an increased need and an increased demand for counseling, both partly due to postwar dislocations and allied problems.

That the "normal" student feels the need for counseling is demonstrated by two studies. The Grant Study at Harvard (16) shows that 90 per cent of the students selected on the basis of good physical, intellectual, and social status had un-

[1] All references are included in the Bibliography, pages 135 to 138.

1

solved problems, 65 per cent in the area of personality. The intensive study made by the Advisory Service at the Merrill-Palmer School and reported in *Women After College* (10) emphasizes that the one hundred graduates interviewed would have been spared much frustration and defeat while in college had they been helped to gain more self-understanding and emotional security. This study also shows that students tended to avoid college counseling services unless they were in serious difficulty, because of the close relationship of those services to the punitive, administrative, or psychiatric divisions of the institution. They would have welcomed counseling under different associations. Professor Melva Lind (23), formerly Director of the French House at Mount Holyoke, supported the view that students are eager for more counseling; she also recognized the dormitory's advantage as a setting for it. She reported that girls ask questions like these: "Why are so many of us unhappy much of the time?" "When shall we begin to feel at ease with strangers?" "Who in college can help us to understand ourselves better?" The studies by Chassel (6) at Bennington College and Howard (38) at Smith College indicated an increase in the number of students seeking help, especially with respect to the number of problems arising from conflict with parents.

DORMITORIES AS CENTERS FOR COUNSELING

Counseling a Function of Residence Hall Administration

Dormitory life offers many opportunities for developmental as well as remedial counseling. It provides students with innumerable clues for self-appraisal in their daily association with their peers. Many opportunities for counseling are also offered in connection with student activities. Properly qualified counselors can offer concrete assistance, not only in self-understanding and solving varied problems, but also in achieving all-round growth and more harmonious relations with associates. That individual development is recognized as a concern of the residence halls program for women students is shown by this statement of policy from a publication of the National Association of Deans of Women: "It is the function of administration in residential life to see that the way is kept clear for the progress of each student toward his best development within the college environment" (33 : 8). Slowly but surely, dormitories for women are coming to be recognized as counseling centers.

Residence Hall Aims Involve Counseling

A residence hall should provide a homelike and congenial atmosphere wherein the shy girl may quickly gain a sense of belonging and the aggressive girl the satisfaction of sharing in cooperative activity. It should help every resident to develop the social skills which make for happier human relations; provide conditions conducive to study and suitable facilities for wholesome recreation; encourage the development of intellectual interests, aesthetic appreciation, and ethical values; give opportunity for the growth of leadership ability and social responsibility through participation in self-government; offer living conditions which foster physical and mental health; and help the student to manage her life with intelligence and self-discipline. In brief, a dormitory should contribute to the student's all-round development, that she may become a socially competent, intelligent, well-balanced person, having concern for the welfare of others.

Residence halls are now recognized as proving grounds in the acquisition of valuable knowledge and skills. By learning to live peaceably and cooperatively with others in the dormitory, students are preparing for the larger responsibilities in adult life (23 : 12).

The dormitories of today aim to provide far more than merely safe and healthful surroundings. The achievement of most of these larger purposes involves effective counseling.

The college campus is the setting for a unique community of girls from a variety of cultural settings, with different viewpoints, interests, and tastes, and bound together by common loyalties strong enough on many campuses to break down barriers of race and social groups. Because the four years in the dormitory constitute a crucial period of transition from the protection afforded by the home to the demands of mature independence, dormitory heads face a real challenge to help each student find herself, establish her values, and achieve an orientation toward the world.

RELATION OF DORMITORY COUNSELING TO THE COLLEGE PERSONNEL PROGRAM

Personnel workers have two general functions: work with individuals, called *counseling,* and work with groups, which includes the social program. The dormitory program embraces both these types of activity. Usually there is only one person in charge of a dormitory. She may be designated as head of residence, dormitory counselor, or by some other title. It is the persons in this position who have more or less responsibility for counseling within a dormitory to whom this book is addressed. Except when reference is made to some of their other functions, their various titles will be used interchangeably throughout, although they have different degrees of responsibility for counseling. A dormitory head or counselor should be concerned with, and skillful in, both of these interdependent aspects of personnel work.

Since the dormitory counseling program is an integral part of the college personnel program, the counseling in the dormitory must be coordinated with that done by other offices. Coordination is facilitated if one person on the campus—dean of men, dean of women, dean of students, director of personnel, vice-president in charge of personnel work, or other official—maintains an over-all view and so organizes the personnel work that it renders maximum service to the students. Coordination among all members of the staff who are serving individual students is aided by the centralization of personnel records. Dormitory counselors should work closely with the faculty advisers, as at Stephens College. They should never feel isolated from the rest of the college. They should meet often with others who work with students on the campus to share insights, pool information, or discuss other professional matters. For example, dormitory counselors can supply enlightening background for the understanding of students who are not working to capacity or whose campus behavior is bizarre. Conversely, they need to know how the dormitory girls function in situations outside the dormitory. Each personnel worker should understand and respect the work of the others. This mutual understanding and respect will facilitate the referral of dormitory students to the persons in the college who have the means of helping them in special ways.

It is often necessary for the head of residence to work through a group or the leader of a group in order to help an individual. Some of the most effective counseling in the dormitory is that done with the student government leaders; they may influence many other students. In their work with groups, both adult and student leaders often become aware of the needs of individual members.

PURPOSE OF THIS BOOK

This book suggests ways in which heads of college residence halls may meet the needs of students through counseling. While it has been written with women's dormitories in mind, much of its content could apply equally well to work in men's dormitories.

Stewart, in her admirable book, *Some Social Aspects of Residence Halls for Women* (44), described the contributions of the social program to the development of social competence, aesthetic appreciation, and democratic citizenship. She pointed out that since students spend one-third of their time in residence halls (not counting the hours spent in sleeping), the environment and the social experiences offered there can be a potent factor in their education. As her book provides impetus and ideas for the improvement of the social program, so this book may contribute toward better dormitory counseling programs.

In view of the interrelatedness of counseling and the social program, it may seem artificial to separate them, as has been done in this book. The reason for doing so is to give more emphasis to counseling, that aspect of personnel work which has received less recognition in descriptions of residence hall work. By focusing attention on counseling and by giving illustrations of real counseling situations, this book may increase understanding of the nature of counseling in the dormitory and may stimulate exploration of its potentialities and the development of improved procedures.

Chapter Two

OPPORTUNITIES FOR COUNSELING

THE purpose of this chapter is to make clear the nature and functions of counseling and to show, by means of concrete illustrations, how favorable a setting for it is provided by dormitory life. The kinds of opportunities will be described.

NATURE OF COUNSELING

Definition

Broadly conceived, counseling may be defined as a face-to-face relationship, usually between two persons, the aim of which is to help the counselee to understand and to accept himself and to gain increasing confidence in his ability to make his own decisions and to choose his goals wisely. Effective counseling will result in desirable changes in the counselee's attitudes and behavior. At its best, the counseling process will be the means of helping him to develop his highest potentialities. Counseling usually involves an awareness of need, the recognition of some problem, or a feeling of stress on the part of the counselee. However, contact with the counselor may stimulate this awareness of need.

Even when only slight modifications in attitude and behavior are brought about by counseling, these may be significant. Every counselor will agree that the solution of a single aspect of a problem or the making of one decision may influence favorably the whole life situation.

Levels of Counseling

One may think of several levels of counseling services. Different kinds of face-to-face contacts may be arranged along a scale, from a request for information at one end, through degrees of increasing emotional involvement, to the psychiatric and psychoanalytic interview at the extreme other end. Needless to say, the dormitory counselor does not have the training to do this latter intensive counseling. The frequent casual contacts which come to a dormitory head in her office, in the corridor or dining room, or at social functions belong on the periphery of counseling. While some of them may be described as counseling, others serve merely to open the way for counseling. The counselor will often effect changes in the environment or encourage social relationships, but this activity on her part is not counseling per se, though it is closely related to it. Nor is the teaching of a skill counseling, important as it may be in an individual student's adjustment. To prevent confusion in terminology, both counseling proper and these peripheral aspects will be included under "work with individuals," in contrast to the social program or group work.

Role of the Dormitory Counselor

Counseling is not synonymous with advising; advice may sometimes be given in the counseling process, but only in response to the counselee's readiness or expressed need. In one sense, the counselor is a co-worker with the counselee. She encourages initiative and independence, rather than dependence. Strang (46 : 107) thus defined the counselor's responsibility:

The counselor serves as a kind of key that unlocks new insights; he is not the center of the counseling process. He listens far more than he talks. He helps to clarify ideas that the student has chosen to bring out into the open. Counseling is "listening guided by understanding"—understanding of the individual and of opportunities for his best development.

Curran (8) said that the chief task of the counselor is to create the kind of psychological atmosphere in which growth is possible. He looked upon the counselor as a catalytic agent.

In the opinion of some authorities, there is a place for giving information as well as for listening, for interpretation as well as for reflection of feeling.

Developmental Character of Counseling

As was pointed out previously, counseling is quite as important for the well adjusted as for the poorly adjusted, since its primary function is to help every girl to reach her maximum development. The real or potential leaders among the students, those who seem to be using their abilities and energy most effectively, are often the most eager for counseling assistance and able to make the best use of it. Sometimes these girls seek guidance in helping other girls to get the most out of college life. Counseling is preventive or developmental, not merely remedial.

The following is an instance of how a student leader was helped by counseling. A student in an eastern women's college worried and felt insecure in spite of the fact that she had been elected to the presidency of a sophomore dormitory. The counselor encouraged her to discuss what she thought were her reasons for feeling this way. The reasons went back to grade school, when she had been dropped (so she thought) by the "gang" because of a rumor that she had said something about one of their members which she really had not said. Thus she felt that she had been unfairly set apart. She had tried not to care and to compensate by excelling in other things. Though she later won recognition in high school as well as in her first year at college, the feeling persisted. Her parents' high expectations for her also exerted some influence. All along, she had the feeling of being unlike other girls, of being more mature in her tastes and in the way she spent her time. Yet she felt that she had no intimate friends. By discussing her reasons with the counselor and getting some insight into why she felt as she did, she was helped materially to gain a different outlook and to achieve more in her work and other activities than she had before.

Preventive Counseling Defended

There are those who say that, except for students in serious trouble, counseling is an unnecessary luxury, who proclaim that *they* got through college healthy and happy without benefit of any counseling services. Such people fail to consider that they might have gained more from college and might later have contributed more to their jobs, families, and communities if they had had this kind of help. These critics of counseling are so imbued with the value of independence that they advocate a strictly laissez-faire policy: any attempt to guide adolescents is an unwarranted invasion of their right to steer their own lives. Since the counseling here described aims to help the student become increasingly self-directive, and since the encouragement of an attitude of dependence is contrary to its principles, their criticisms are not well founded.

THE DORMITORY AS A FAVORABLE SETTING
FOR COUNSELING

Informal Atmosphere

The dormitory has certain advantages as a setting for counseling. In the first place, the approach to the students can be lifelike and informal. The atmosphere of the head of residence's living room and of the dormitory lounge or office is one in which students are likely to feel relaxed and responsive. Especially in a small dormitory is it possible to build a warm, friendly relationship between students and the head of house. Students may linger to talk in her office or room while waiting for the mailman. At those times, the contents of letters are often shared, and intimate hopes or fears are voiced.

A dormitory head writes of one such case:

Marion came in to tell me of her happy surprise at receiving a check for $10 from her mother, who had been worried about her daughter's apparent lack of energy during her week end at home, and wanted her to take a week's rest from her part-time job in the cafeteria. The girl was so pleased because now she would be able to attend some social functions which conflicted with her scheduled time on the job. I encouraged her to talk about herself —her dates and extracurricular activities, her job and study load. As a result, Marion decided she had been attempting to do too much and that she would take a week's rest from some of her social activities as well as her work. She then planned to budget her time to conform to her energy, economic limitations, and academic ambitions.

A chat after dinner around an open fire may lead to a serious discussion of personal matters. Sometimes a detail in the furnishing of the counselor's room plays a part. For example, a girl who had been unresponsive and somewhat negative in attitude showed an unusual admiration for a small piece of original Greek statuary. The counselor learned that the girl had great appreciation for, and knowledge of, art. She was later able to have her put in charge of the art bulletin board, a step which helped to change her attitude toward other people and toward the college. In this informal atmosphere, the counselor knows the girls as individuals, and they, in turn, respond to her as a friend.

Unlimited Opportunity for Observation

The dormitory counselor has the chance to observe the girls in a great variety of situations. She sees how Mary reacts to the frustration of having a week end spoiled; how Jane treats, and is treated by, her family; how Jessie presides at house meetings; how Sally entertains her boy friend; how Greta seems always to be alone. When the girls come in from evening engagements, their responses to what they have seen and done are often illuminating. Sometimes a play or a movie which has impressed them will evoke a serious discussion of values. At teas during the examination period the dormitory counselor notices which students are tense or depressed, which appear to work hardest, and which are perhaps procrastinating because a recent examination gave them a "lucky break." When faculty or distinguished guests are entertained at receptions or teas, she learns which girls need help in making conversation or in introducing people graciously. Or she may note that Helen, who waits on table, appears worried; she may later discover that this is owing to fear of not having sufficient funds to continue in college and resentment over lack of time and money to buy attractive clothes for dating. She at once becomes aware of the change in Bernice who, happy and radiant last year, is now beginning to be seclusive and absent-minded, and she ponders over a number of possible causes. Because she knows Bernice so well, she is able to recognize that a definite personality change has taken place and to help her decide to consult a psychiatrist for the professional help the counselor realizes she is not competent to give. She rejoices that Emma is developing self-confidence as a result of her successful leadership in the Debating Union; that two roommates have learned mutual tolerance; that Grace, who used to call her family by long distance telephone every night on the most trivial pretext, now does so only on special occasions. Thus the dormitory counselor is in a strategic position to sense possible needs and to appraise growth.

In a small dormitory, when the head of the house passes by the girls' open doors she will often be invited in to admire a new rug or to share a box from home. She can learn much about the personalities, interests, and habits of the girls from observation of their rooms. (This does not mean room inspection, which is better done by someone else.) If there are roommates or suitemates, she can note their interrelationships.

Apropos of the value of observation, a dormitory head who is doing effective work with 107 residents writes this:

I have often found it possible to discover a situation before it assumes tragic proportions. I try to be constantly alert for the student who does not fit into the house group: the one who has no friends (she may be shy or definitely objectionable), who goes from table to table before she finds a seat, the small group of two or three who do not mingle with the others, or the student who is exceptionally untidy about her room or person.

Many Kinds of Needs

The dormitory counselor has a chance to deal with many kinds of needs, some of which may give rise to extended counseling. For example, when crises develop, as when a girl gets word that her fiancé has been killed in a plane crash or when another girl gets the dreaded news that she is in danger of being dropped by the college because of her poor work, the counselor is on hand. Perhaps she notices that Nancy looks unusually tired as she signs in from a week end. By making a friendly inquiry, she finds that Nancy's parents are planning to be divorced and that Nancy has been unable to sleep because of worry over the consequences to herself and to her mother. The girl is relieved to be able to unburden herself for some minutes. Later, she will return for help in facing the issues involved and in deciding what part she ought to play. When a student feels that she has been the victim of an injustice, she will feel free to "blow her top" to the counselor if the right kind of relationship has been built up. Jane, whose parents have forbidden her to marry Ed because of his different religious and cultural background, comes in after a telephone call home, depressed and worn out by the conflict between her loyalty to her family and her love for Ed. Sarah, a freshman about whose strict upbringing the counselor knows, returns late with her date, very garrulous and slightly under the influence of liquor. Later, when she talks with the counselor about her home and previous experience, she is able to look at her situation of the previous night and discuss the values involved without getting on the defensive. She decides, of her own accord, that she will refuse to go out with this escort unless he promises to stop drinking.

Another instance in which understanding brought better results than immediate disciplinary action is given in a letter from a dormitory head in a western college:

Helen came to my attention during her sophomore year because of her very untidy room and person, with resulting ostracism. I asked her what the trouble was. She thereupon broke down and told me a long tale of a summer love affair abruptly broken off by the man. For several weeks she had been in a complete slump, paying no attention to her room, her personal appearance, or her academic work. On further investigation, there appeared to be family trouble adding to the turmoil. In this case, it was necessary to work with the college psychiatrist, her dean, a member of the faculty, and her brother. My part was mainly to stand by, ready to listen to her at any time and to encourage her until she finally worked out her problem.

How unfortunate it might have been if this state of affairs had not been uncovered when it was!

The counselor may sometimes see unusual behavior which reveals a need for counseling. For example, early in the year a counselor in a large dormitory noticed that a certain girl who had been assigned to her table in the dining room sat hunched over her plate, not entering into the conversation and replying only in monosyllables when directly addressed. The counselor invited her to her room, and later the girl gained enough confidence to discuss her deep feelings of inferiority. The same counselor noticed that another girl, instead of entering the dining room and standing with the others at the table until all were ready to sit down, as was the custom, continued to sit and read in another room. Meeting her later in the hall, the counselor commented on this behavior; she found that the girl was frantically using every free minute for study because her time was taken up by the rehearsals and performances of the five orchestras to which she belonged. She claimed that she could not continue at college without the money she earned in this way. She resented the time she had to spend in the dining room, would have preferred a lunch counter, but could not spend the extra money. This was a situation requiring extensive counseling and modification of the circumstances. It occurred at a large residence unit in an urban college.

In the informal atmosphere of the residence hall it is difficult to draw the line between chitchat and counseling; one merges into the other. For example, the counselor was chatting with a girl who had had a rather serious emotional upset the previous year: a counselor on whom she had developed a "crush" had left the college suddenly. This girl now talked at some length about a girl living on her corridor whom the counselor had suggested she might be able to help. Then she remarked that she felt herself such a different person this year. She believed she really was growing up. The counselor helped her to evaluate the change. The girl said she had learned not to become so emotionally involved in her relationships with others; she also felt she was less dependent on her mother. She had learned not to place so much importance on "pleasing the professor"; she was now working chiefly out of interest. So she went on. The counselor was partially engaged with some business that could not be neglected at that time of day, but she listened sympathetically as the girl thought things through herself. Because a good relationship had been built up as a result of previous counseling contacts, it was possible for this friendly conversation to take on the character of real counseling.

Sometimes, out of situations which arise in meetings with student planning committees or the student government organization, the counselor arranges conferences with leaders who need help in working more smoothly with people or in handling disciplinary problems with tact and fairness. These student leaders sometimes come to realize that they themselves have inner conflicts or environmental handicaps which keep them from being effective. In many colleges, the liberalizing of social rules and the increasing student responsibility for their formulation, enforcement, and interpretation free the counselor from her disciplinary role and make it possible for her to be a co-worker with the mature girls in helping the less mature to become cooperative members of the community. On the other hand, this increased freedom also enlarges the scope of the problems these leaders must meet. For example, in colleges where there are unlimited late permissions one must reckon with their effect on the girls who have not yet learned to achieve a balance between work and play, and with the reaction of this excessive social life on the other students who share in the preludes and postludes to these evening engagements.

General Adjustment Problems

The dormitory is thus an ideal place for the making of personal and social adjustments: how to live with others, especially in the same room, how to take responsibility for the care of one's possessions, how to study near a constantly busy telephone, how to manage one's day efficiently, how to assume social responsibility, how to practice democracy, how to live within one's allowance—adjustments of almost all kinds, simple and complex. Occasionally a student's family may thwart the achievement of some of these learnings. For example, the head of a large dormitory found that a family maid was being sent in every few days to straighten out one girl's personal effects, press her clothes, and do her errands. In this case it was necessary to explain that the girl could not continue to live in the dormitory unless she could learn to do these things for herself. Both counseling and the teaching of certain practical techniques were involved here.

Flexibility of Scheduling Interviews

There is one other advantage of the dormitory as a setting for counseling. Interviews may be informal and spontaneous or scheduled at a definite time, as needed. They are less subject to administrative restrictions than in other college offices; that is, they can be held in the evening when the girl feels less hurried and when there are fewer interruptions from the telephone. Interviews can usually be relatively lengthy if it seems desirable; there is less likely to be a waiting line, such as one often finds outside other offices. Hence, the dormitory counselor can be at leisure and accessible, thus encouraging consultation that might not take place otherwise.

NEED FOR COUNSELING AS EXPRESSED
BY DORMITORY STUDENTS

Three studies have been conducted by the writer in a residence unit of an urban non-denominational college housing about 350 students—studies motivated by the need to find out what the students expected from dormitory counseling. The students in this college are younger but higher in intelligence and in general more independent and mature than those in many women's colleges.

Investigation with Transfer Students

Interviews with twenty-five transfer students from as many different colleges indicated that their greatest need for counseling in residence halls had been in connection with social relationships, especially with men and with roommates. When asked what the head of residence had done that was helpful or what they felt she could do, they replied as follows:

Promote mixing between classes and cliques.

Encourage the student government officers to take more leadership in aiding new students.

Help the girls to realize the advantage of developing an attitude of give-and-take.

We need help in seeing the other person's viewpoint, and from that we can develop consideration of others.

The head of residence should see that there are adequate social outlets for the girls. This is probably the most important of all, since other problems stem from a lack of this.

The head of residence should talk to both girls where there are roommate difficulties and try to work out the problem with them.

The engaged girls talked to the head of residence about marital adjustment; the others, about men in general.

The head of residence was able to introduce suitable men to the girls who didn't know any.

The house mother greatly aided those girls disappointed in not making a sorority.

Academic difficulties were next in frequency. The girls spoke of these in rather general terms as "study problems," "choosing a major," "finding time to finish assignments," "worry about grades," "trouble choosing courses," "quiet hours not respected by others, so that it is hard to study," "trouble with roommate over studying together." When the girls were asked to be more specific in describing their study problems, they seemed unable to do so, either because the problems were not really of as great concern as they claimed, or, more likely, because no one had ever helped them make any sort of analysis.

Less frequently mentioned were the problems of making vocational plans and of thinking through one's philosophical and religious ideas. Probably the students found help in these areas outside the dormitory. One girl spoke appreciatively of a head of residence who acquainted the girls with job requirements and opportunities. Problems connected with the home situation and health and emotional problems were mentioned by very few. Two girls who had been shocked by the death of a friend spoke of the dormitory counselor's helpfulness. Resentment at dormitory restrictions and money troubles were apparently minor matters in the experience of these girls.

Questionnaire Given to Seniors and Sophomores

The statements obtained in the interviews mentioned above were used to make up a questionnaire designed to investigate more widely students' counseling needs and attitudes toward counseling, and to gather suggestions for the improvement of dormitory living. The questionnaire consisted of two parts: (1) questions to which free responses were asked, "How can a residence hall director or her assistants best serve the students? What should she *not* do?" and (2) a list of fifty possible functions for a head of residence, most of them related to counseling, each of which the girls were asked to evaluate on a five-point scale ranging from "is of primary importance" to "should not be attempted." (See Appendix A.) The questionnaire was administered to students of the senior and sophomore classes, in most cases during interviews in which the students were encouraged to comment freely and frankly upon the various statements to make sure that they understood each.

The results of the questionnaire were not treated statistically, since the girls' comments and their responses to the question quoted above were considered more significant than the numerical weighting of the items. However, it was evident from an analysis of the data that the girls felt it essential to have in a dormitory a friendly and sympathetic adult who knew and understood students and with whom they might discuss any personal matters frankly and without fear of criticism.

The girls said that it was important for the dormitory counselor to help them to feel "accepted" and to have a sense of "belonging." They also stressed their need for aid in the improvement of the techniques for all sorts of social contacts. They suggested that help be given indirectly through frequent small, informal parties. One girl said: "Meeting men friends is very important to happiness." Another said, "The most important thing the counselor can do for a girl is to help her make at least one close friend." However, concern was expressed lest a girl suspect that she was being "sold" to others. One girl, who said that the need for social experience could be taken care of by a student's close friends, was stumped by the query: "What if she has none?"

Most of the girls stressed the importance of being treated as individuals in matters of discipline. One girl put it: "You can't and shouldn't treat all offenders alike, except in small matters. Especially in unusual cases, you must consider the needs and background of the girl." Another girl, a student officer, agreed, but recognized the need for some consistency and order. She ended by saying, "This is a tough problem."

Nearly all the students felt that it was extremely important to work cooperatively with the head of residence on plans to make their life in the residence hall successful, harmonious, and pleasant. This, they said, should include the working out of rules and provision for their enforcement.

A majority expressed a desire for some assistance in deciding on a vocation. They felt that guidance in this area would encourage a girl to get more out of college. One girl remarked that help in choosing and finding a summer job might contribute much toward the making of a vocational choice. Others felt that this function was handled adequately by other offices in the college.

About half the students were in favor of receiving help in the analysis of their study habits and use of time. Typical remarks: "Wish someone freshman year had done that for me." "Girls should be helped to realize the scarcity of time and the value of doing away with non-essentials." About remedial reading: "A slow reader will find college very arduous." About help with study habits: "A little late. It should have been done in prep school." "Important only if a girl is having a lot of trouble." Regarding help in scheduling time: "College life is so full of activities and of unexpected happenings that, though ideally desirable, it is not very practical."

Only about half thought it necessary to help students in assuming social responsibility, or to give assistance to the leaders of student government. Perhaps these items (numbers 22 and 33) were worded infelicitously, since certain girls expressed the opinion that the student government should be free from faculty interference, although they agreed unanimously that students and administrators should work together in all matters.

"Help in religious orientation and development of a philosophy of life" seemed to suggest to many of the girls a definite program of action, instead of counseling contacts to be initiated by the girls. Many felt that this aim could be achieved through their courses and through contacts with people and all kinds of experiences, or that it was the function of the home, church, school, or chaplain. Some thought, however, that the head of residence could help by encouraging "bull sessions" and by showing an interest in religion and a willingness to talk about these things.

The reactions of the students to the item, "help the girls to achieve independence from their families" was a rather personal one, depending on each girl's relationship with her parents. Some girls felt strongly that this help was needed. One girl, whose mother seemed to be around frequently, emphasized her approval by putting three exclamation points after the statement. Somewhat more than half felt with equal vehemence that counseling along this line should not be attempted, because it was too touchy a subject ("Leave family relations alone!"), because they did not desire independence, or because they felt they could achieve it by themselves. One rather mature girl said that she would like help in achieving "at least a satisfactory new relationship."

Among these students there was a wide difference in attitude toward counseling. The majority indicated that they considered help desirable and necessary with reference to most of the functions included in the questionnaire. Some students qualified their opinion as to its desirability by warnings against hovering over the girls. One girl remarked, "Try to 'feel a girl out' to be sure she isn't just being reticent about talking and really wants help." Another student, with reference to item 14, "encourage girls to speak very frankly by not passing judgment on their conduct," cautioned, "Try to avoid the antagonism a person sometimes feels afterward toward the person to whom she has spoken very frankly." A typical comment was, "Many girls feel that they would like to talk to an older person about their affairs or things that trouble them." A very few indicated a general state of insufficiency. One girl said that she felt most girls were very independent and resented guidance as interference. She felt that a social program was needed more than individual counseling.

The investigator tried to make it clear to the students that the chief purpose of the study was to discover in which areas they thought they or their fellow students would be likely to seek assistance. Despite this explanation, a few apparently had in mind a kind of spoon-fed guidance. Without exception, however, they took the investigation seriously and responded thoughtfully and in detail. In addition to giving general information on needs for counseling, as the students saw them, the study had the value of revealing the individual problems of some of those interviewed. The investigator recommends the use of such a questionnaire as a means, not only of provoking discussion and interest, but also of getting acquainted with students who have seemed inaccessible to counseling.

Freshman Study

Another study was conducted with eighty-six freshmen in the same college soon after their arrival in the fall. They were asked to write a reply to the following question: "If you had felt the need to talk to some older person soon after you arrived, about what would you have liked to talk?" Sixteen were unable to think of anything they had wanted to talk about, though they cooperated by checking the second part of the questionnaire.

Those who replied mentioned forty-six items that can be classified as academic. For example: "advice on length of study hours"; "detailed explanation of requirements for degree so that I can plan courses ahead"; "I find that I must spend almost all my time studying and have little time for anything else" (an overconscientious, painfully shy girl who may have been using study as an escape); "the feeling of being over my depth and awfully ignorant in classes—a complete change from high school"; "difficult to study because people don't keep quiet hours"; "great change in marking system and attitude of professors from high school—more impersonal and demanding"; "sometimes I feel lost in the transition to the great amount of studying I must do"; "trouble keeping my mind on my work"; and "talk with someone about my courses at greater length." The item most frequently mentioned was the difficulty of finding out how much time, relatively, should be spent on study and other activities. It was not surprising to find academic problems most prominent in this college, where there is considerable stress on academic standards, especially at the beginning of the year when freshmen are likely to be confused by the number of demands made upon them. On the other hand, a few freshmen felt that the academic work of college was easier than that of boarding school.

The girls mentioned only twenty-six personal–social items. Among these were a desire for help in getting on with people, especially roommates, and needs to gain more self-confidence, know how to meet boys, and learn to be open-minded toward attitudes met in fellow students. One mature girl wanted help in finding out the best ways to assist others who were having a difficult time. Another wanted to know what to do about a boy friend who drank and thought anyone a "sissy" who did not also drink.

A few interesting quotations will make these items more explicit:

Being a foreigner, I am not accustomed to some of the customs of the country, and I don't believe in accepting a date from a boy I have met once or twice. Is it rude not to?

I'm afraid I still have the feeling of being an extremely small part of the college.

It is rather difficult when you come to a new place to get adjusted socially.

I could have used advice in developing a certain amount of poise and self-confidence.

I'd like to talk about the natural tendency to miss home and old friends.

Seventeen items had to do with dormitory rules or life in the dormitory. Since freshman late permissions are restricted during the first semester, it is natural that several should have wanted to discuss the possibility of additional permissions. A few girls asked why the system of assigning seats in the dining room could not continue to function throughout the year, since this practice breaks up small closed groups or cliques. Others complained about girls who did not respect quiet hours. There were various housekeeping grievances.

Fifteen items had to do with general adjustment to college life and to the city. Many of the girls wanted help in choosing activities or clubs. One girl expressed a desire for a single long paper, instead of several separate sheets, listing all the events she needed to go to and miscellaneous information she needed "about everything in college": a new sort of digest!

Only nine items were vocational. A typical response to these: "I am so far very undecided about my career and do not want to take the wrong courses for whatever I do decide to do."

Some of the students may have felt that the questionnaire was a check-up on the effectiveness of the dormitory orientation program, to which they had just been exposed. A number commented favorably on it: "everyone helpful—felt at home right away"; "completely happy as to dormitory life"; "surprisingly easy to adjust—and for one who has had difficulties before"; "everything so well organized that I didn't feel need for help."

When the investigator later learned more about the girls as individuals, their comments took on a new significance. For example, one of the most mature, later elected class president, spoke of the bewildering feeling she got in thinking that she was really taking on the responsibilities of adulthood: "This is a thought which comes only naturally to girls entering college where for the first time they are plunked down in an impersonal sort of system, where they must shoot for themselves, so to speak." A very young girl spoke of being overwhelmed by the amount of work required and by the impersonality of the college. She wanted reassurance which would "make problems seem smaller, not larger." A very gregarious girl wanted help in planning her time, so that she would not fritter it all away. A girl who later showed a need to impress adults because of a feeling of insecurity expressed a desire for an "evaluation of my abilities, character, and talents—and the planning of an ordered procedure in bettering character."

COMMON STUDENT PROBLEMS

For her observation of students, the writer has found the following to be a few of the problems common among freshmen:

1. Having to supervise personally one's own activities without being checked on, as at home.

2. Feeling lonely because one is afraid at first to talk confidentially to new friends.

3. Finding oneself a little frog in a big pond, the opposite of the situation in a small-town high school.

4. Finding out that college is not so glamorous as one imagined.

5. Trying to decide what to do about an unlikable girl who sticks close.

6. Wasting too much time in "bull sessions" and bridge games, and then letting work pile up because there is no check-up in class.

7. Resisting the temptation to ask advice about many details from a roommate, as one did from family at home.

8. Not being able to figure out "what the professor wants."

9. Finding it hard to compete with girls who have had wide social experiences.

To the girls these seemed important causes of frustration at the time, trivial though many of them appear to be.

The writer attempted to classify the counseling needs revealed in her interviews with dormitory students over a two-year period, but concluded that any figures giving relative frequencies would be meaningless since many of the problems were multifaceted and since the problem seen by the student often turned out to be merely a symptom of a deeper need. The general area of personal–social relations, usually with an emotional background, seemed to be predominant; for instance, worry over family troubles, especially divorce; conflict with parents over marriage or other critical decisions; tendency toward withdrawal owing to feelings of inferiority; tendency toward daydreaming and procrastination; too great dependence on family; fear of taking the initiative in talking to people at social affairs; inability to make oneself liked, because of personality handicap; emotional disturbance at being dropped by a boy friend; conflict due to difference between one's moral standards and those of certain associates; lack of self-control resulting in constant friction with roommate. These are not difficult to classify, but what can be said about the following: desire for scholastic perfection carried to an extreme; lack of purpose on the part of a very able student, resulting in poor work; chronic inability to concentrate? These are not purely academic problems, by any means. In *Women After College* (10) the point is made that there is no such thing as a discrete problem, since each must be met in relation to the total life of the functioning human being, and every phase of personality or experience affects, in varying degree, the whole person. Perhaps this interrelationship of the different aspects of a problem can best be illustrated by the following example, a type of counseling situation that is especially common in dormitories where the counselors are members of the faculty. Here, it will be noted, academic, social, and financial factors predominate. A dormitory counselor wrote:

A freshman came in recently for advice about her major field. She had come from a small-town high school where she had been valedictorian of her class and one of the leaders in extracurricular activities. Her work here has not been up to standard, and her social adjustment has been poor. She has few friends and has not been able to indulge in extracurricular activities because (1) she lacks self-confidence in social situations, and (2) she feels that she must spend all her time on her academic work. The situation is complicated by her need of scholarship aid (which probably will not be forthcoming because her academic rating is low) and by the fact that she feels that she has failed her school, her family, and the college by her lack of success.

On the whole, she seemed philosophical about the situation when she talked to me, and she said repeatedly that she had hopes of doing better the rest of the year. She reported that she was getting to know more people—and she was having more fun than she had had earlier in the year. She seemed to think her methods of study were improving. I discussed various methods of study with her, as they applied to different types of work. We discussed the methods of meeting people and of entering into activities. We talked of possibilities for a major field of study based on her own special interests and her vocational aims. Then we talked over plans for the future if she should find herself unable to return next year for lack of financial assistance. I tried to point out to her that I thought she had gained a lot from her year here —and that no one could take this gain from her. This idea appealed to her and she began "on her own" to enumerate what she thought she actually had gained. She began to take a more hopeful view of the future and saw that, even if she could not return here, she could still continue in various ways to prepare for her chosen line of work. She seemed to feel pleased with her plan of study for the spring term as we had worked it out. I felt that I had helped her to gain some perspective on her problems, and had helped her to see that things had not been a complete failure: that there was definitely something that she had gained from her experience, hard as it had been for her. It is too soon to say what the real results of such a talk may be. The outcome can be evaluated only in the future.

SUMMARY

This chapter has first of all explained the counseling process and the role played by the counselor. It has focused chiefly, however, on the dormitory as a center for counseling: the opportunities it presents for counseling, the chances it affords the counselor to observe and study the student in situations

that are peculiar to the dormitory, and the kinds of needs
which arise there. Three investigations have thrown some
light on counseling needs, as reported by the dormitory students of an urban college. However, the complexity of most
problems met in the dormitory makes any rigid classification
of them almost impossible.

Chapter Three

KNOWLEDGE NEEDED BY THE
DORMITORY COUNSELOR

In view of her opportunities for counseling as reported in the last chapter, the dormitory counselor should have a special background of knowledge and understanding. She will always be concerned, first and foremost, with particular individuals, each one different from every other. However, she should also know, on the authority of others as well as from her own experience, the influences which help to shape youth, their basic needs, the adjustments peculiar to their age level, and the characteristic problems of certain groups. She should understand the seemingly irrational behavior which people unconsciously adopt to meet frustration, and should be able to recognize the symptoms of serious maladjustment. She should be aware of her own limitations. And obviously she will need detailed knowledge of both the social and academic aspects of the college environment.

INFLUENCE OF THE CULTURE ON ADOLESCENTS

Unstable Mores and Values

American youth in these mid-century years, depending somewhat on the section of the country and the type of community and family from which they come, are affected by shifting social mores. Some girls are faced with choices and decisions which would not have existed for a previous generation. Their parents, confused about their own values, lacking a sense of direction, and uncertain about the maintenance of their own authority, evade responsibility by telling their

daughters to use their own judgment, though they have not
helped them to form a basis for making that judgment. Instead of building self-reliance, this practice may actually increase the girls' feeling of insecurity. Granted the need of
youth to rebel a little against family "old fogyness" and community conservatism, young people also have a right to know
that their parents possess certain relatively stable moral values
and standards of taste.

Characteristic Goals of Our Society

Youth are also affected by the goals which seem to be characteristic of our society. Landis (22) named these as follows:

1. Competition-success, in social life, school, and business.
A study made by Loomis and Green (26) of a typical state
university campus emphasized the high social prestige attached
to making the best sorority or fraternity, being able to date
attractive members of the opposite sex, being elected to office,
and the like. They said that the ability to get high marks is
respected unless the student is known to work too hard or to
be a social reject. In other colleges, competition for high
marks assumes more importance. Examples of competition
in communtiy social life and the vocational world are too
familiar to need citing. Conflict with parents over a suitable
mate may result from this preoccupation with "success."

2. Individual freedom and self-expression. Young people
have a strong urge to be original. In our culture, it is relatively
easy for them to be different from their parents. But since the
achievement of adulthood is facilitated by identification with
parents, too great a striving for dissimilarity may complicate
this adjustment. Some young people place such a high pre-
mium on freedom from restraint that they hesitate to consult
adults lest they be bound in some measure. Where individualistic self-expression has been overstressed, social values are
likely to suffer.

3. Standardization, the opposite of the previous goal.
Campus mores and fashions exert strong pressure on the col-

lege student to conform. It takes a brave soul to defy the current vogue for ragged dungarees and worn-down "scuffies."

4. Sensuous enjoyment. Magazine and radio advertising fosters a cult of comfort and pleasure. The idea that personal happiness of a rather limited sort is all that matters in marriage is also prevalent. Landis' study (22), showing that 67 per cent of adolescents from sixteen to eighteen practice "necking," possibly indicates that in our society romantic love may have come to be used as a compensation for isolation, as evidence of success in social relationships, or as a means of restoring an individual's self-assurance. This explanation seems to have some point, in view of the competition in the dormitory for dates and the frequent feeling of defeat over lack of them. Some of the least well-adjusted girls seem to have the greatest "need" for excessive "necking," seem to be almost anxiety-driven toward it. Despite their seeming poise and self-assurance, some of these young people bear out Zachry's characterization of adolescents (60) as restless, unsure of themselves, and a little scared.

Conflict Between Roles of Homemaker and Career Girl

Kamarovsky (21) reported another cultural conflict that affects some college girls today: they are uncertain whether they want the role of homemaker or that of career girl, and cannot decide to devote themselves wholeheartedly to either. Society seems to be expecting them to undertake both, but they cannot envisage doing justice to both.

Uncertainty of Society about Adolescent's Role

Linton (24) made an interesting point about the role of the adolescent in our society. He said that in cultures which recognize adolescents as a distinct group with suitable activities of their own, they have no difficulty in making the transition to adulthood. Two possible alternatives, he said, are either to treat them as children or to treat them as adults;

and both are bad. The one thing worse is what we sometimes do in our culture: leave their social role uncertain; that is, demand submission and obedience one minute and expect them to assume the full responsibility of adults the next. Adults, amazed at the vagaries of youth, often say that adolescents want all the privileges and none of the responsibilities of the grown-up. Perhaps adolescents are not entirely to blame for this.

BASIC NEEDS OF ADOLESCENTS

Because adolescents are in the transition stage to adulthood and to the achievement of social status, the following needs assume special importance for them:

1. **Need for recognition and respect.** To feel valued as a person, to be esteemed by at least a few others, is of great significance to an adolescent. The less recognition a girl has had in the past, the more exaggerated is her present need for praise. Constant criticism by family and teachers increases this hunger.

2. **Need for group acceptance, a sense of belonging.** With many adolescents, perhaps with most, this need for recognition by one's peers is the most critical requirement. Being a member of some group engenders a feeling of security, of identification. Relationships of this sort are of tremendous importance in the formation of values. Adolescent attitudes are much influenced by organized and by informal group activities.

3. **Need for intimate response and happy social interaction.** Satisfying contact with peers of both sexes is very important. At this period, friendship seems to mean more than in later years; at least, it is more demonstrative.

4. **Need for experience and expression.** Creative activities provide an emotional outlet. Sometimes they give a meaning and focus to life. Religion, too, is a strong integrating force.

5. **Need for individual achievement and success.** As was mentioned above, the need for material success has been ac-

centuated in our culture, sometimes to a pathological degree. Through the influence of the college environment and through counseling, a girl may broaden her concept of success and achievement.

The acquiring of emotional and social maturity is facilitated by satisfaction of these varied needs. The underdeveloped egocentric who has no interests outside her own circle; the girl with a brilliant mind who feels no responsibility for using her intelligence constructively; the overdependent person; the shy, retiring girl who is unable to make social contacts; the habitual evader and procrastinator; the non-comformist, who sees no reason for any dormitory regulation—all are expressing unsatisfied needs and trying to find satisfaction in devious, "expensive" ways. Even such a selected group as college students may be showing the effect of previous frustrations. Anyone with experience in working with dormitory students will recognize the importance of the satisfaction of normal human needs.

MAJOR ADOLESCENT ADJUSTMENTS

Gaining Independence from Home

One of the major adjustments which must be made by the college student, and especially the freshman, is gradual emancipation from family ties. This adult independence will not be complete, even after college, so long as the girl remains financially dependent; in fact, it is doubtful whether it is ever quite complete. There is considerable variation in the degree of this achievement among college freshmen. Some girls, competent and poised, come to college alone, and thereafter seem to manage their lives efficiently and smoothly. One such girl, the writer once noted, was encumbered for a few days after the opening of college with a mother who could not seem to tear herself away. Her daughter obviously did not need or even especially want her; the girl simply went about her business of getting settled and making friends, being as polite as she could be to her mother and never actually ignoring her. Another freshman might find it very hard to say good-by to her mother. She would be delighted to have her stay on to make her curtains and choose her program of courses and clubs. This sort of mother might telephone the head of residence from several hundred miles away to demand that her daughter's roommate be changed, though the daughter had not even complained to the head of residence. A girl so dominated may find it hard on her own responsibility to get to classes on time and to organize her day. She will probably call her parents to consult them before making the smallest decision. Perhaps they will foster this dependence by driving to the college every week or by urging the girl to spend her week ends at home. Still another girl may be so annoyed at the way her parents watch over her and check up on her that she will adopt the sort of behavior which only redoubles their possessiveness. There is likely to be a student in the group who is so eager to run her own life that she avoids all adults in authority lest they, like her parents, try to control her. For this reason, she does not ask for counseling assistance even when she needs it badly. Occasionally, there will be a girl who is in open revolt against her family, even to rejecting all their values. She may transfer this hostility to others in authority, and thus resent the counselor's friendly interest in her. Lastly, there is the girl who feels that no one, not even her parents, can understand her. This attitude may possibly be a projection of her own lack of understanding of herself. Just as parents need to understand that when a girl withdraws, she still needs their help, so must those *in loco parentis* recognize and accept the feelings of this student and try to show her that it is natural for adolescents at a certain stage to exhibit some negativism toward parental demands; that this is a part of their effort to establish their independence; that there may be times when they will want to be both independent and dependent.

Still another kind of adjustment to the process of becoming independent of one's family was reported by a dormitory counselor in a small university. A freshman, older than the others because she had worked some years prior to entering college, was much upset because of her father's opposition to her attending college. He had even gone so far as to tell her she could not return home because she had gone against his wishes. Her mother was in full accord with her desire for a college education, but her father dominated the household. Evidently he resented losing the financial support she had been giving, although he was quite able to support the family without her assistance. Meanwhile, he vented his wrath on the mother and sisters, even going so far as to refuse to work at all. Undoubtedly, he was mentally ill. The girl had to work long hours to finance her education; this took time away from her studies. She was constantly worried by her family situation and felt partly responsible for the trouble they were having. Fortunately, she was able to talk to others about her worries and had the kind of personality which won her many friends. She was gradually helped by her friends and counselor to see that there was nothing she could do to change her father's nature and that she was not helping her family situation by her worry.

Establishing Heterosexual Relations

Another major adjustment, that of achieving heterosexual relations, is frequently made before the student enters college. However, there are always a few girls who avoid association with boys and appear to have no interest in them. Perhaps one of these students will seem to have a sort of fixation at the tomboy level, an unwillingness to grow up and to face the realities of adult life. This resistance may be related, in some cases, to the girl's need for emancipation from home; in others, to her unwillingness to accept a feminine role. Greater opportunity to associate with men tends to decrease homosexual behavior in women's colleges. This is a complicated problem

and there is no space for the extended discussion it needs.
Other girls are compulsively eager to meet men, but never
seem able to hold their interest. Still others exhibit "approach-
withdrawal" tendencies, either because they lack social skills
or because they have experienced some sex miseducation.
A few, sometimes those with well-developed intellectual interests, lack the social facility and small talk which would help
them to get acquainted with boys. Perhaps this is because they
have no brothers or have always gone to girls' schools. They
may feel that college boys are too immature to be interesting,
and may crave an opportunity to meet older men. Being un-
successful in their efforts to do so, they plunge the more avidly
into student activities. Then there are the girls, unfortunately
more numerous today, who will try out anything in their relations with boys; they lack not only decent standards, but any
understanding of the connection between mere physical expression and the deeply satisfying aspects of married love.
The majority of the girls will probably make a normal adjustment; the above are a few of the difficulties which can be ob-
served in a dormitory.

There will be all degrees of sex knowledge, too, even in
this "sophisticated" age. As compared with previous genera-
tions of college students, more girls will have received sex
information from their parents as well as from their peers.
However, despite present-day frankness of speech, if one may
judge from the attendance at voluntary lectures at a liberal
arts college and from the range of questions asked there, information is by no means fully disseminated. One student,
while filling out the question described in Chapter Two, expressed surprise at the meagerness of the sex knowledge of a
few of the girls on her corridor. Students' thinking about sex
covers a considerable range, from unwholesome attitudes of
fear or disgust and unsocial attitudes of indulgence or nar-
cissism to mature attitudes toward love and marriage. Finally,
there are differing standards with regard to behavior with
men and "petting." The mature, experienced head of resi-

dence will find a challenge to do her most expert counseling in this realm of attitudes and values. The inexperienced counselor may do better to refer a student to someone else for this kind of assistance.

Finding the Self

In these transition years when selves need to become integrated, many girls become concerned about developing some sort of personal philosophy. As Elliott (9) put it, a girl "must somehow build the uncoordinated desires and impulses of her being into a dynamic whole that will have unity and purpose." At this time, a girl may worry because she feels as if she were several different selves and does not know which one she wants to be. She needs to understand that this is all a perfectly normal part of the growth process.

With some students, this search for unity in life will take the form of religious doubt or metaphysical speculation. Perhaps, as Elliott (9) suggests, this questioning is closely related to one's need to find her own place in the universe. The writer has noticed that about the sophomore year, philosophy and religion courses become popular. A girl will say, "I don't quite know why I'm taking this, because it's not related to my major interest in any way, but I thought it might help me to settle a lot of questions I've heard discussed." A few students brought up in very orthodox homes are disturbed by these courses, as well as by some in the field of social science. This kind of conflict is emphasized in the interviews reported in *Women After College* (10); the interviewees tended to cling emotionally to their earlier, traditional views, and yet intellectually to reject them in the light of their new ideas. There is need for a concerted effort on the part of the faculty members to help such students integrate these new and disturbing ideas into some sort of coherent philosophy. Here is a fertile field for guidance.

Certain groups in college maintain a pose of cynicism toward any sort of quest for a central meaning to life. Perhaps it is not fair to say, "pose," though sometimes a girl may cover up a sensitive, idealistic nature by a cloak of cynicism. On the other hand, a poorly adjusted, unhappy girl may say, as one did to the writer, that no world is worth living in but an artistic world: "Why would anyone *want* to be like the people one sees around her who can adjust to ordinary life, with all its ugliness and sham?"

In his study of a state university, Loomis (26) maintained that religious and philosophical values have no place, and that students' attitudes are little changed by the courses they take in college. On the other hand, the extensive study, *From School to College* (13), indicated that there is evidence of considerable change in students' thinking about their philosophy of life. Though there was less interest in formal religious observance, more than half of the students surveyed in the latter report indicated that they had gained religious insight that gave their lives new significance. The writer's observation in two liberal arts colleges supports the view that students do have a concern about their place in the universe. One girl has a strong feeling that she wants to use her abilities to raise the status of the underprivileged by working in remote rural districts; another is deeply concerned about the prevalence of racial prejudice and the rights of minorities. One southern girl says that she came to a northern college because she hoped to have some association with Negro students, but is disappointed to find so few. Another speaks of the battles she has waged in the dormitory against the prejudice of a few of the girls. Others are eager to do rehabilitation work in Europe or to serve as missionaries. Some feel that through political, civic, or religious work in their own communities, or by means of teaching, social work, or medicine they can contribute in a small way to making a better world. It is probably true, in many colleges, that there is less overt interest in religious observance and even in the discussion of religious matters than formerly, except where there is dynamic leadership. Can this be, in part, due to the fact that we live in an age in which meditation and reflection are difficult, and in which the adults with whom adolescents associate talk little of religion? Someone has said that whereas in a past age people felt inhibited in talking about sex, in this age, they appear embarrassed when the subject of personal religion is brought up. The potentialities exist, however, for a widespread search for spiritual values.

Finding a Vocational Goal

Dormitory students say that they gain more from their college experience when they have at least a tentative vocational plan. Anyone who has counseled students knows that a common cause of below-capacity achievement is lack of purpose. Then, too, mental health is fostered by the sense of direction which comes from having thought the matter through and decided upon a vocation. A girl's happiness after college, unless she marries immediately and never faces the need for self-support, depends to an important extent on her being prepared to enter a suitable vocation. In fact, choosing and entering upon a vocation are such vital elements in the process of finding the self that a girl who has never met the test of self-support has perhaps not attained full maturity.

Achieving Good Mental and Physical Health

For some students, learning good health habits is an adjustment of major importance. There seem to be several groups who have difficulty in this area:

1. Those who neglect themselves through carelessness or ignorance.

2. Those who neglect health needs because the feverish pursuit of social or extraclass activities is more important to them. These girls omit meals, stay up most of the night, and neglect to report when ill lest they be sent to the infirmary and hence be unable to attend the prom or take part in the play.

3. Those who are carrying a burden of remunerative work that makes it almost impossible for them to prepare assign-

ments and still live a well-balanced life with time for recreation and rest. These students sometimes feel frustrated because
they find themselves at a disadvantage in the competition for
dates. In some institutions, happily few, they may suffer some
social discrimination. Thus, on several counts, they may be
in danger of mental ill health.

4. Those with special health handicaps—cardiac conditions,
polio, diabetes, serious defects of vision or of hearing—who
for one reason or another need special consideration. Some
of these girls, because of the wise attitude of their parents, will
be among the most self-directive of the student body; others
may have developed almost an invalid complex.

5. Those who tend, consciously or unconsciously, to use
poor health as a means of evading responsibility or unpleasant
consequences. A girl may be able to dream up a nervous condition which requires a couple of days' rest in the infirmary
just at the time of an examination for which she is not prepared. The dormitory head should recognize the psychological factors which may be involved in such cases. Examinations
are sometimes emotional crises, even for good students. It
requires considerable acumen to understand the dynamics of
behavior operating in such a situation. Ill health may also be
an attention-getting device as well as a means of escape: there
is the girl who plays a sort of martyr role, who insists on doing
everything, despite the fact that she feels "just miserable."
She may enjoy the pity which she excites.

Dormitory heads have the advantage of being able, through
observation, through chance remarks of other girls, and
through contacts with parents, to learn much about the actual
health habits of each girl, especially those pertaining to eating,
sleeping, care of the eyes, exercise, cleanliness and general personal care, worry, and the care of colds in their incipient
stages. The girl who does not go down to dinner, but who
later in the evening eats two frankfurters and an ice cream
soda; the girl who arises only ten minutes before class, with no

time for breakfast and certainly no time for developing proper habits of elimination; the girl who seems to be in perpetual motion, both emotionally and physically; the chain-smoker whose badly bitten nails suggest extreme nervous tension; the untidy, even ill-smelling girl who is shunned by others; the physically lazy individual who cuts gym regularly and never exercises voluntarily—these are in need of counseling.

An illustration of the relation between bodily functions and psychological factors may be found in obesity. In some cases there is evidence that emotional factors, especially guilt and anxiety, may be the cause. Excessive eating serves as an escape from the anxiety aroused by separation from overprotective parents. The writer once tried to counsel a girl who was an overindulged only child. She seemed unable to meet any difficulty, and habitually lied to avoid unpleasant consequences. When the writer suggested that she might make up in summer school the work she was consistently failing, despite good ability, she burst into tears; her mother would never let her study like that in the summer! She spent her evenings in purchasing and consuming quantities of food. Her sole comforts were in eating and in talking to any willing listener about her family and home town.

Meeting the Academic Demands of College

In every group canvassed, a sizable number of students mention worry about academic work as a major cause of strain. This is especially true of freshmen because they have to adjust to new methods of teaching, rapid and selective note-taking, more difficult subject matter and more extensive reading, higher standards of marking, essay-type examinations, and the lack of a daily check-up. They are also being introduced to such complex activities as weighing the evidence offered by two conflicting authorities and writing term papers. Some students sum up the whole difficulty as one of "finding out what the professor wants," especially in answering examination questions and in writing themes. More mature students are stimulated by this challenge and by the opportunity to develop mentally. Many, especially the less able and those who come from high schools with low standards, are discouraged. The dormitory counselor should not spend so much time with this latter group, who seem to need help more, that she neglects helping the more able group to find the satisfaction of genuine intellectual effort.

If a student of fair ability who has weathered the first year successfully begins to have constant difficulty with her work, emotional factors are likely to be present. For example, fear of failure may be connected with excessive parental pressure. Lack of sustained effort or fear of talking in class may have its roots in a feeling of inferiority in comparison with a brilliant and successful sister. Excessive dependence on precise directions, or such overconcern with details as results in neglect of a clear over-all view of a matter, may also have an emotional basis of guilt or anxiety in connection with family relationships. Chronic inability to concentrate and habitual procrastination usually indicate the presence of some conflict. Of course, a sudden drop in the quality of a student's work may be the result of a temporary emotional upset. For example, a student officer who had previously taken great pride and interest in her work suddenly began getting low marks. The girl confided that she had had a severe shock just before examinations: the young man whom she had hoped to marry had suddenly broken off relations with her because he had fallen in love with one of her best friends. Pride had kept her from talking to anyone about it; hence she had been unable to concentrate in class or to study. The work of another girl had suffered similarly because she had been upset by malicious gossip concerning her relations with her boy friend.

Adjusting to Marked Differences
in the New Environment

Besides the difficulties of academic adjustment, new students, especially freshmen, meet other frustrations. For example, many girls come from a relatively stable environment to one which presents, in addition to the general confusion of newness, the possibility of a number of untried adventures. A girl from a protected home in a small community may experience her first contact with a more sophisticated type of girl who knows her way around and who has somewhat different values. Especially in colleges where there are sororities, students often fear not being able to hold their own socially. For many students, this social competition is a greater source of anxiety than scholastic competition. In the study, *From School to College* (13 : 57), one of the most common problems reported is "finding it difficult to be oneself because one is tempted to seek above all else social approval." The very multiplicity of activities from which to choose may tempt girls to scatter their energies. Some freshmen go to the opposite extreme; they rationalize their lack of outreach by the statement that it is better not to go out for any extraclass activities until one has found herself scholastically; yet they spend considerable time playing bridge with the girls from their own preparatory school. Freshmen who have been "big shots" in their high school feel deflated when they cannot play a major role in the dramatic organization, when their stories do not rate with the campus literary editor, or when they are not nominated for a class office.

Sometimes the adjustment to a roommate or suitemates is the critical factor. Different standards of housekeeping, different habits of sleeping and studying, different temperaments and tastes—such differences can be bridged only by maximum cooperativeness on both sides. Considering the many hazards of living with a stranger, students often display amazing adaptability and mutual tolerance. With almost unlimited unscheduled time at their disposal and with freedom in cutting classes and the possibility, in some colleges, of dating every night, perhaps the chief hurdle for the freshmen is to learn to run their lives efficiently. The girls who come from the most regimented boarding schools are often at a special disadvantage; happily, some of these schools have recently been experimenting with the granting of more freedom. The dormitory counselor can help her girls to use their time and energy wisely, to find greater satisfaction in their social relationships, to meet disappointments philosophically, and to gain a more mature set of values.

SPECIAL ADJUSTMENTS REQUIRED
OF CERTAIN GROUPS

Transfer Students

In some colleges, transfer students are the "forgotten women." While they may not need quite the same kind of orientation assistance as do the freshmen, some of them may require more help with social relationships, since their classmates will already have established themselves in social groups. Transfers are also handicapped in taking a leading part in student activities because they are not known to the student body as are those who entered with the freshman class.

Women Veterans

The women veterans fall into somewhat the same category, though they have special problems of their own. Many have not studied or taken examinations for several years; hence their reading and study habits are rusty and they find it hard to get used to an academic regime. Some have had no previous college training, perhaps not even a full college preparatory course in high school. Maturity and seriousness of purpose, however, usually compensate for these lacks. Indeed, these young women sometimes find their classmates immature. As a reaction from army or navy regimentation, they may find college rules irksome. In the writer's experience, they welcome assistance in making the most of their college years. Many of them have had vocational experience as well as service in the armed forces; they have a keener realization than the average student of their own needs and lacks.

Foreign Students

Though foreign students, who are numerous in some colleges, are a picked group who usually make a successful adjustment to college, they, too, have some special needs. There are, of course, enormous differences among them in language facility and in general adaptability. Our manners and customs shock those who have had conservative upbringing, unless they have had previous contacts with American young people. Some have financial difficulties: their expenses here are greater than they had anticipated and it is almost impossible for them to import money from abroad. In some cases, since only a small group of their countrymen can hope to receive the benefit of higher education, they find it hard to understand how girls here can take education so much for granted. Those who suffered great privations during the war find us very frivolous. Our system of accrediting courses often makes it difficult for them to finish training before their funds run out. These girls are eager to make contacts with Americans, and they dislike being thought of as a special group. However, the less secure among them welcome a chance to talk with older persons who know and appreciate the different sort of culture from which they come.

Minority Groups

Students belonging to racial and religious minority groups experience difficulty only when there is an undemocratic spirit; fortunately, that is rare on college campuses. When they feel insecure or different, these students are likely to limit their associations to their own group and perhaps to compensate by being either overcompliant or overaggressive. A few may show oversensitiveness to criticism; they may feel that they alone are being singled out or discriminated against in some way. Others may be under strong pressure from parents to achieve academic success, in order to raise the family status. Those whose parents have not assimilated our culture and have tried to bring their daughters up very strictly may experience considerable conflict, especially in giving approval to their daughters' choice of men friends.

Highly Gifted Students

Students with very superior ability or talent in some special field sometimes find it hard to "suffer fools gladly"; they may develop the habit of impatience with the slower mental processes of others. Those who have not been encouraged in high school to realize that they have a responsibility to contribute their talent to the group have highly individualistic attitudes. Their academic work may be far below capacity because they do not feel challenged. Their development may be one-sided because they work only on subjects which excite their curiosity. Rather than exhibiting impatience at their shortcomings, the counselor should realize that these girls need sympathetic understanding quite as much as do those of less ability. It is a special challenge to the dormitory counselor to help those who have high ability to make their maximum contribution and hence to derive the fullest possible satisfaction.

The Problem of Grief

Sometimes a student who suffers the loss of someone very close to her experiences a feeling of guilt as well as of grief. She may appear to make a quick adjustment, to take up her activities normally. Then suddenly, after a lapse of months, she has a breakdown; the severe repression of her grief is taking its toll. This is a difficult problem which may require psychiatric help. It can be prevented if the girl's friends and her dormitory counselor encourage her to express her sorrow and to talk freely about the loved one at the time of the bereavement. If her family is one which considers any expression of emotion unhealthy, she may resist this help. Of course, the dormitory counselor must know the girl well enough to understand what the loss means to her, if the most effective help is to be provided.

The Student Who Develops a "Crush"

A student who gets a "crush" on the dormitory counselor presents an especially difficult problem. The counselor must ascertain just what relationship the student is seeking with her. Is she to be a mother-substitute for a girl who has experienced deprivation, who is not well adjusted socially, or who has had an abnormally hard time breaking with home? While she needs to avoid becoming emotionally involved herself, she cannot rebuff the student who has a strong need for such a personal relationship. The counselor can do a great deal for the girl if she is wise enough to help her understand why she feels as she does. If she does not have this skill, she had best refer her to someone with more training in psychological counseling. However, since the counselor is the strategic person in the situation, she must be sure that the referral does not indicate rejection to the girl. (See also the later section on referrals.)

These few special groups have been cited, not with a view to setting them apart or labeling them "different," but to make certain observations about them which may or may not apply to given individuals. Though girls like these may never give the dormitory counselor cause for concern, she should be aware of their possible needs.

UNDERSTANDING OF ADJUSTMENT AS A RELATIVE TERM

The counselor should recognize that what is good adjustment for one individual may not be good adjustment for another. For example, a girl may achieve a degree of independence that is commendable for her, though it consists only in the ability to make a trivial decision such as whether to go away for the week end. Asking the professor a question in class may represent a real victory for one girl, whereas for another, asking questions may represent an undesirable attention-getting device. Moreover, adjustment is seldom permanent; in fact, it is a continuous process. The same problems tend to recur in different guises. In the case histories reported in *Women After College* (10), this fact is strikingly apparent. In counseling with students, the head of residence should help them to understand their individual differences in adjustment and to focus attention on their individual progress toward a more satisfying use of their energy and abilities.

MECHANISMS FOR MEETING FRUSTRATION

The dormitory counselor should also be familiar with the common means which people have of meeting frustration. These are often called "behavior mechanisms." Only an uninformed person will think there is no explanation for irrational behavior. Though a girl who behaves in a certain way may be her own worst enemy, her conduct has a certain logic if one can understand its unconscious motivation. That is why argument or persuasion is usually futile. For example, a girl may habitually transfer blame to others because that is more comfortable than bearing guilt or taking responsibility for mistakes herself. The most common instance of such behavior occurs when a girl blames the professor for a low mark because she does not like to face the guilt of her own neglect. Or she may constantly criticize in others the faults that she is unaware of, or the tendencies that she fears, in herself. A compulsive need for high academic achievement may be compensation for a feeling of inferiority which stems from lack of social acceptance. A girl of inferior attractions or attainments may find satisfaction by identifying herself with her brilliant and socially competent family. The writer knew of such a girl who talked constantly of her brother's accomplishments and seemed unwilling to make any effort to change herself.

As was suggested earlier in the chapter, some girls use illness as an unconscious device to get attention or as a means of avoiding responsibility. To cite an example of this: A girl of rather high ability who came to college against her wishes (she had wanted to go to art school) missed half her examinations because of colds. Each time a make-up examination was set, especially in a subject that she had neglected, she would again become ill.

For a painfully shy girl, withdrawal from all competitive activity may be a means of avoiding pain. Some girls substitute excessive daydreaming for successful achievement. On the other hand, aggressive, boisterous behavior may sometimes partially satisfy a drive to dominate. Occasionally a girl will exhibit compulsive behavior by being meticulous to an absurd extent or by appearing disturbed when her ritualistic way of doing something is disrupted. Perhaps the most common means of self-protection is giving "good" reasons instead of the real reasons for doing something. Justifications for extravagant purchases are often of this nature. The devices a girl uses to lessen her frustration will, in general, be those which in the past brought relief from tension and other satisfactions. Bingham (3) said that we need to study a girl with a personality handicap to determine whether her basic pattern is avoidance of persons and situations, the projecting of blame, fear of change, or some other self-protective device. It may or may not be wise, in the course of counseling, for the counselor to make the girl aware of her defenses; it *is* important for the counselor to try to understand them. However, it is dangerous to draw conclusions too quickly, and it is always more useful to describe and try to understand behavior than to label it.

RECOGNIZING SYMPTOMS OF SERIOUS MALADJUSTMENT

While a dormitory counselor cannot safely make a diagnosis of mental disorder, it is important for her to know some of the clues to, and symptoms of, serious maladjustment. To be sure, it is difficult to draw a line between normal and abnormal behavior; there is the danger that the naïve student of abnormal psychology will look for pathological conditions that do not exist. Still there are a few danger signals which might lead one to look for further evidence: a marked change in behavior persisting over an extended period; extreme seclusiveness; erratic, bizarre behavior, especially with stereotyped mannerisms; slow movements and much sighing; chronic sleeplessness and lack of appetite; evidence of severe tension while carrying on a conversation, shown sometimes by badly bitten fingernails or areas of skin badly scratched; frequent confusion in thinking; constant inappropriate smiling; persistent feeling of being the target of derogatory remarks; excessive overconcern regarding health. Where clues point to a single girl as being responsible for constant stealing, especially for no logical motive, one may, of course, suspect kleptomania. In all cases where observation seems to warrant it, the logical next step is referral to some specialist. This will be discussed in the next chapter.

COLLEGE MORES AND STUDENT LIFE

The college mores and traditions, the student organizations and clubs, and the student activities in the community constitute an important area of knowledge and, in a large institution, a complex one. By occasionally attending open meetings and performances, by inviting campus leaders to dinner, and by reading campus publications, the head of residence can get her knowledge at first hand. The importance of college mores in shaping student thinking and attitudes cannot be overestimated. Those cohesive but informal groups known as cliques have an especially important influence, at least on their members. The dormitory head must know their composition, the extent of their influence, and what they stand for. She cannot help knowing a good deal about the social life of the girls through her own observation. She should be familiar with the cultural resources of the college and, moreover, with those of the surrounding community, which, in the case of a large city, will be rich and varied. Thus she will be able to share the enthusiasm of the girls for certain pictures in a museum, for a new play, for the works of a certain composer, or even for attractions such as the exotic food of a foreign restaurant. Since counseling never takes place in a vacuum, the head of residence needs to know as much as possible about these varied influences.

THE MOST IMPORTANT KNOWLEDGE

No matter how extensive the dormitory counselor's knowledge and understanding of all these environmental and psychological facts about students in general, it is useless unless she knows each individual student. This means that she must have not only the easily obtainable facts about each one, but also the more intimate kind of information that is obtained only through skillful counseling. Obviously, she will need first of all to learn the complete names of new students as quickly as possible, no small task in a large residence hall. The mere act of addressing a new student by name, simple though it is, helps to make her feel that she belongs. The ability to fix names and faces quickly is not so much a special feat of memory as the result of keen attention and persistence.

The following chapter will take up some of the techniques of studying and assisting the individual student in the dormitory. There will be a brief treatment of the dormitory counselor's responsibility for educational and vocational guidance. Since knowledge of the college curriculum and of other academic matters, of vocations and of appropriate places to get information about training is an intrinsic part of educational and vocational guidance, it, too, will be treated in the next chapter.

Chapter Four

ESSENTIAL COUNSELING TECHNIQUES

THE first step in counseling procedure is to study the individual student: her abilities, her interests, her present and past environment, her special needs. The counselor will get this information from observation of the student in the dormitory, from interviews with her and with others who know her, from tests which the counselor administers, and from records kept in the personnel office. The counselor will assemble these data in a cumulative record folder for each girl, and periodically she will synthesize the most relevant facts in each case.

OBSERVATIONS AND THEIR RECORDING

Counselors probably differ widely in their ability to observe accurately and to interpret what they observe correctly. However, most of them can acquire these skills through practice, provided certain factors are taken into account. For example, the counselor should beware of basing conclusions on a single dramatic incident. She should be aware of the halo effect: the tendency to respond favorably to the student whom she likes spontaneously, and the opposite tendency to allow her total judgment to be prejudiced against a girl who has offended in one respect. She should consider the psychological setting of each observation: whether the girl is showing off or feeling shy in the presence of particular persons.

To guard against lapses or inaccuracies of recall, the counselor should have some convenient method of recording her observations soon after they are made. A loose-leaf notebook is a good medium, for the sheet or half-sheet on which she has written can then be dropped into the girl's folder. Her recording should be selective; otherwise, the folder becomes cluttered with irrelevant material. Each observation should be dated. A single observation may be recorded as follows:

Mary Brown
(Hall or dormitory)   October 15, 19—

Noticed Mary (a freshman) dressed flashily and with more conspicuous make-up than usual, engaged in animated conversation with young man in hall. When the night watchman indicates that it is time to lock up, she and her escort ignore him. Presently, a student officer intervenes, to remind her. Mary glares at her and seems to be telling her that it is none of her business. However, she accompanies the man to the door where there is a long farewell and tight embrace.
Behavior—typical
Interpretation: Mary does not get along well with the girls on her corridor, who complain that she is a show-off and has crude manners. Her father and stepmother are conservative people of Italian background who speak little English. Is Mary, in acting in a manner that would shock her parents terribly, merely asserting her independence of the sort of upbringing which she feels is not modern? Is there resentment and feeling of rejection at her father's remarriage? Has she transferred this resentment to others in authority?

Studying the behavior of a girl while she is taking a psychological test or answering the questions in a personality inventory is an instance of planned observation. Studying a succession of individuals in a uniform situation is more scientific than unplanned observation. However, it is not necessarily more useful.

CUMULATIVE RECORDS

Policy varies from one college to another as to the amount of information on each student which needs to be kept in the dormitory files. Few residence halls have complete personnel records, especially in cases where the head of residence and the counselors have access to centralized files. Duplication of effort should be avoided. The size of the residence unit, the accessibility and adequacy of the centralized records, the time at the disposal of the counselors or secretaries for keeping complicated records, and the degree of their professional training are factors determining the nature of dormitory records. In *Residence Halls for Women Students* (33) the authors pointed out that it is a mistake to set up an elaborate system of records unless there is enough use of the material to warrant the undertaking. The primary purpose of such records, from the standpoint of the counselor, is to reveal something of the individual girl's capacities and needs as an aid to better counseling. They should never become an end in themselves. However, as Strang (46) stated, the very act of keeping records directs the counselor's attention to individual students and may set goals for both counselor and students.

A common practice is to keep in the dormitory file a folder for each student containing, typically, the personal data card, recorded and dated observations and interviews, correspondence with parents and others, and the rating sheet on which the counselor or head of residence makes a personality estimate of the student for the dean.

The Personal Data Card

A convenient form for recording personal data is a large cardboard blank folded to fit the file. It may consist of three parts:

1. Information on the student's previous home and school background, including such items as her parents' education and occupation; her health record; her school record and the results of aptitude or other tests; her own interests, activities, talents, and goals, as indicated during her school years.

2. Information regarding her achievement and adjustment during college years: for example, her vocational plans and work experience; her academic record; her extraclass activities and offices; her college health record; her adjustment to dormitory life; descriptions by faculty members of her personality

and work habits; the names of her roommate, faculty adviser, and student adviser.

3. Ample blank space for summarizing observations made by counselors, interviews with the student, and self-appraisal by the student. Here at the end of the year a summary paragraph may be written which will present a useful picture of the individual. Residence hall heads and their assistants must exercise great care in the drawing up of this blank, since, for reasons of finance as well as of continuity, revisions cannot be made often.

The precollege information for this card may be secured from the admissions office if its records are sufficiently full. Large residence units sometimes send their own blank to the student to fill out before she enters college. The answers to such questions as "What do you hope to get from college?" or "What experiences have been most significant in your development and what persons have influenced you most?" often provide illuminating indications of the girl's attitudes and needs. She may reveal herself as much by what she does not say as by what she includes. The fact that those who use this information in the dormitory may draw up this special form precisely to suit their needs, makes it particularly advantageous.

Other Records

Other dormitory records have significance in the study of the student, apart from their function of facilitating contacts with her. Some of these are:

1. The daily schedule card of classes and activities filled out by each girl.

2. Week end or overnight permission blanks. These, when tabulated, show the extent of a girl's absence from the campus and the persons and places she has visited.

3. The social card showing the number and nature of the girl's evening engagements and when she returned. If these

records are kept, they can be summarized for each resident.

4. Records of participation in dormitory activity, kept up to date by the girls themselves. These include the names of students who serve on committees, take part in skits, concerts, or art shows, make posters, pour or serve as hostesses at teas, canvass, take guests around the campus, and assume other responsibilities. These records make it easier for the head of residence to spot the girls who are not getting the social experience they need, as well as those who are carrying too much social responsibility.

5. Room inspection slips filled out by the housekeeper, indicating the condition of the girl's room.

6. Room application blanks (made out in the spring). Since these show, not only the names of the girls chosen as roommates, but also the names of those near whom a student wishes to room, they provide data which might be used for a sociometric study.

Case Study

The relevant information in a student's cumulative folder is sometimes supplemented and synthesized to make a case study. This is a more comprehensive record, useful when a student is having considerable difficulty in adjustment or is working far below her capacity.

Interpretation of Records

The dormitory counselor must, of course, know how to interpret the information on the girl's school record. For example, she must be able to read between the lines when evaluating teachers' recommendations and students' and parents' statements. The interpretation of test data requires special knowledge. For instance, since different group intelligence tests yield different IQ's, it is necessary to know something about the various tests. A single IQ from a group test is of less value than a Stanford-Binet or Wechsler IQ. It is desirable to know how a student's IQ compares with those of her classmates, a piece of information that is unfortunately seldom given. The counselor should be able to interpret the percentile ratings that are commonly used on school records. For example, a percentile rating of 50 indicates that the student excels fifty out of every hundred of the group with which she is being compared. It is necessary to know the group with which the student is being compared. For example, one student may have a percentile rating of 80, according to the national norms; that is, only 20 per cent of all the students to whom the test was given in the same year of college made higher scores than she. If she is in a school in which the level of intelligence is very high, her percentile rating according to the school norms may be only 60, whereas it might be 80 according to the average score of students in the same class in the total population tested. The counselor will need to know what raw scores (verbal and mathematical) on the Scholastic Aptitude Test given by the College Entrance Examination Board are considered average by the college, and what the range of scores was in the particular case. She should know that L-percentile rating and Q-percentile rating on the American Council Psychological Examination refer to linguistic and quantitative achievement respectively.

The results of reading and other achievement tests may be reported in terms of grade scores (G-scores). For example, a G-score of 11.2 on a reading test indicates achievement as good as that of the average student who has been in the eleventh grade for two months. Again, the results might be based on either national norms or school norms. One point requires special emphasis: a single low score on any test may not be significant, but a high score usually is significant. In other words, the student *can* do at least as well as the high score indicates; she *might* be able to do considerably better than the low score if the test were given again under more favorable conditions. Since an extended discussion of test interpretation is outside the scope of this book, those who wish more information on the analysis of test results, including the use of such measures as standard deviations and standard scores, are referred to recent books on tests and measurement.

TESTS IN THE DORMITORY PROGRAM

The preceding discussion of the responsibility of the dormitory counselor for interpreting test results leads naturally to a brief consideration of tests as part of the dormitory counseling program. Obviously, the need for tests will depend in part on the nature of the total college counseling program. That is, where there is an adjustment clinic prepared to give tests on the campus or where some other office or department has that function, the dormitory counselor will not need to administer tests. Many colleges have a general testing program, in which such tests as the American Council Psychological Examination and the Cooperative English Test are given to all students, but make no provision for individual testing. Under these conditions there is value in giving certain individual tests in the dormitory as an integral part of the counseling process, provided, of course, that a member of the residence halls staff has the necessary specialized training.

The matter of competence in the administration, scoring, and interpretation of tests deserves considerable emphasis. Some tests require only the mastery of printed directions plus a little practice. Others, such as the Wechsler-Bellevue, require a period of supervised training. The interpretation of the results of some tests may be learned from a careful study of the manual; of others, only by clinical experience and with the help of a supervisor. If tests are not given under standardized conditions, scores cannot be compared with the norms. For example, in the administration of a group test like the American Council Psychological Examination, split-second timing and exact phrasing of the directions given by the tester are essential. With individual tests, maximum rapport between counselor and student is required for valid results. If the dormitory counselor does not know the uses and limitations of tests, she may give a false interpretation of the results. For example, the results of the Strong Vocational Interest Blank administered at age sixteen may not hold at age twenty. The Meier-Seashore Art Judgment Test samples only one small part of the complex of abilities called artistic talent. The Strong and the Kuder Interest Inventories do not sample precisely the same things; the former purports to measure the interests of the student indirectly by comparing his responses with those of a large number of successful people in certain vocational fields, while the latter obtains scores in broad areas of interest, such as the literary or scientific. The self-descriptive questionnaires, such as the Bernreuter Personality Inventory, measure group trends with some reliability, but should, according to Super (49), be used with caution for individuals. Because tests are fascinating to most people, there is danger that an untrained counselor may yield to the temptation to use them without knowing enough about them.

Use of Tests

Tests should never be used as a substitute for counseling; their function is to aid the counselor in understanding the student and in helping her to appraise her strengths and limitations. Tests which measure interests, special or general abilities, and attitudes can give information that is useful in making educational and vocational decisions. Such self-understanding is often valuable in personality adjustment. The writer recalls a very able girl who had been doing only mediocre work and had felt discouraged because she thought she could not do more. She was also somewhat diffident in manner and did not make friends easily. The test results gave her new confidence in herself so that she was able to do work of a quality that gave her satisfaction. She then changed her vocational plans from medical secretary to doctor, thus acknowledging a secret ambition which she had hitherto felt was unattainable. Fortunately, the shift was made early enough to enable her to plan her courses appropriately. Like the pebble which makes an ever-widening circle when dropped into the water, the knowledge that she had considerable ability permeated her whole personality: she became more purposeful and more outgoing. This change improved her relations with others, and their more favorable attitude in turn increased her confidence even more. Possibly other factors entered in, but the precipitating cause seemed to be her knowledge of the test results.

Tests furnish the trained counselor with valuable clues to the nature of the girl's personality; she can observe and analyze her behavior during the test and study her oral and written responses afterwards. This is especially true of individual tests, such as the Wechsler-Bellevue Intelligence Scale. A good reading test which has diagnostic value and well-established norms for college freshmen may help a student who is having trouble with some of her courses to locate the source of her difficulty, so that she can take remedial measures. Vocational interest tests assist a student in identifying her interests and may throw some light on her personality. The foregoing suggestions cover some of the ways in which tests may be used in the dormitory counseling program. It follows as a matter of course that reports both of significant observations and of objective test results should be put into the student's cumulative record folder.

Tests should seldom be given unless the student requests them; they may interfere with counseling by setting up a barrier. Testing should never be separated from counseling; if it is used as an isolated technique, there is danger that it may become an end in itself, rather than a means to an end.

Which Tests?

In this book there is space to mention only a few tests. The reader is referred to books on tests and measurement and for a critical evaluation of many tests to Buros' *Mental Measurements Yearbook* (5) for information about others.

As a measure of scholastic aptitude, the American Council on Education Psychological Examination for College Freshmen[1] is a good test because its results correlate highly with college scholarship. The fact that it yields both a linguistic score and a quantitative score makes it useful in educational guidance. Recent research by Anderson (49) showed that the L-score alone correlates highly with academic success in a liberal arts college.

The Wechsler-Bellevue Intelligence Scale[2] (55), as mentioned above, is an individual test yielding a verbal IQ and a performance IQ. Though its five performance tests have a low correlation with academic success on the college level, they reveal much about the personality and have certain vocational implications. From observation during testing one may learn something of a student's attitudes toward others, her methods of work, her language facility, her ways of reacting to frustration, her ability to plan, her confidence in herself, her emotionality. Norms are available for the individual subtests as well as for the total verbal and performance scores. From these, it is possible to make a limited diagnosis of particular abilities. As was pointed out above, this test must be administered only by a trained person. It takes over an hour to administer.

For appraisal of a student's reading, the Cooperative English Comprehensive Test 2[3] is excellent. The Nelson-Denny Reading Test[4] takes less time to administer and is self-scoring, but it gives less information about various kinds of reading responses.

There seems to be conflicting evidence as to the diagnostic value of the self-descriptive type of personality test, wherein the testee responds, "Yes," "Sometimes," and "No" to a series of personal questions. Two that have been widely used are the Bernreuter Personality Inventory[5] and the Bell Adjust-

---

[1] American Council on Education, 744 Jackson Pl., Washington, D. C.
[2] Psychological Corporation, 522 Fifth Ave., New York 18, N. Y.
[3] The Cooperative Test Service, 12 Amsterdam Ave., New York, N. Y.
[4] The Cooperative Test Service.
[5] Psychological Corporation, 522 Fifth Ave., New York 18, N. Y.

ment Inventory.[6] Their main shortcomings are their suscepti-
bility to faking under certain conditions and the ambiguity of
both the questions and the answers. Furthermore, they aim
to measure only certain limited aspects of personality. Nevertheless, these tests may be used as a tool in counseling; the
questions may stimulate the testee to see connections between
areas in his life or to sense attitudes in himself, the perception
of which may lead to genuine insight.

The Rorschach Test justly claims to reveal the underlying
personality structure which makes behavior understandable
and is therefore considered the most valuable of the personality tests. Since it takes years of study to learn to interpret the
results, it is obviously not a practical test for the dormitory
counselor. However, its administration is not so difficult to
learn, and it is possible to send the results to an expert for
scoring and analysis. This is expensive, but might be worth
while for a small number of students.

Of the vocational interest tests the Strong Vocational Interest Blank[7] is probably the best-known. It is more adequate
for men than for women. This test reveals the similarity between the testee's interests and those of persons actually engaged in a limited number of occupations frequently chosen
by college students. It shows whether, given the ability and
training, he is likely to enjoy that kind of work. Its validity
has been fairly well established by extensive research. One
drawback is difficulty of scoring; it must usually be scored by
an agency such as the Educational Records Bureau.[8] One
should not try to interpret it without first having made a thorough study of the manual and some perusal of the research.
The Kuder Preference Record[9] is a promising and helpful
test. In this test, students' responses are grouped according to
general areas, such as mechanical, scientific, literary, and per-
suasive, rather than according to specific vocations. A chart

[6] Psychological Corporation.
[7] Stanford University Press, Stanford University, Calif.
[8] Educational Records Bureau, 437 West 59th St., New York, N. Y.
[9] Science Research Associates, 1700 Prairie Ave., Chicago, Ill.

is supplied showing the occupations in which these general aptitudes are important. The Kuder test has the advantage of being self-checking. Both the Kuder and the Strong tests are self-administering. In analyzing results on either of these two tests, the counselor should consider low scores as well as high; she may also make use of some of the actual responses themselves. A third test which is useful in vocational guidance as well as in personality analysis is the Allport-Vernon Study of Values,[10] which aims to measure the relative prominence of six basic interests or motives: the theoretical, economic, aesthetic, social, political, and religious. It is both self-administering and self-scoring.

Special aptitude tests, such as musical, clerical, or mechanical, are not practical for dormitory use. Aptitudes for most vocations likely to be followed by college graduates do not lend themselves, because of their complexity, to measurement by tests.

How Test Results
Should Be Given to Students

Most students are eager to know the results of tests. The practice which some institutions follow of withholding all information deprives the student of a means of self-appraisal. A student needs an opportunity to evaluate her assets and liabilities intelligently and to become objective about her limitations. However, the manner in which the information is transmitted is important. Because IQ's are so frequently misunderstood, it is better not to give the actual figures but to say: "You did better than 90 per cent of the general population and you are above the average of your own class." If a student has done poorly, one may say: "Your score was below the average of this group on this particular test. It might be that you would do better than that if tested another time. However, though your score is low in comparison with those of some of the others here, remember that the differences are

[10] Houghton Mifflin Company, Boston, Mass.

not great in a college group. Also, this test measures only one aspect of what is called intelligence, and you have other assets which may have more to do with success than this." Students who have been struggling with courses too difficult for them are often able to face their limitations philosophically, and are relieved to have a change of program which lessens the strain. The counselor will use her knowledge of the girl, especially of the girl's attitudes toward herself, to decide how much she will tell her and in what manner. The dormitory counselor may sometimes discuss frankly with a student some of the behavior observations which she has made in the test situation; frequently, such a discussion will lead to further counseling. For example, a counselor pointed out to a girl who had just taken the Wechsler-Bellevue Test that she always seemed to want to criticize her own responses. The girl said she had not been aware of that and wondered what made her do it. She said she thought she was that way in class recitations and in talking to strangers; she was always afraid she might have said the wrong thing. This observation led to further discussion which was helpful to the student in getting insight into her lack of self-confidence.

The counselor should always keep in mind the necessity of looking at test results, not in isolation, but as one means of understanding more about a complex personality.

EDUCATIONAL AND VOCATIONAL GUIDANCE

This discussion about cumulative records and tests forms a background for an examination of the dormitory counselor's responsibility for educational and vocational guidance, and of the specialized knowledge that should be hers for the discharge of this function.

In some colleges the dormitory counselor merely supplements the work of other personnel officers in assisting the student with her educational and vocational plans; in others, she may have the major responsibility. Whatever the extent of her responsibility, she should have the necessary knowledge and skills. More than half the students in a college where the administrative offices took care of this function felt that there was need for supplementary help in the residence halls. There are usually too many students for any one office to counsel adequately. One freshman said to the writer, "I realized, of course, why it was not possible for me to talk to my adviser as long as I wanted, for there were others waiting." Moreover, a few girls may find it easier to talk to a dormitory counselor; this is especially true in cases where vocational choice is complicated by a personal problem.

Administrators are beginning to recognize that educational guidance and vocational guidance are part of the same process. There is no one time during the college course when all stu-ents should make vocational plans. However, the necessity for choosing a major at the end of the sophomore year usually forces the student to do some thinking on both phases of the subject.

Knowledge of the College Curriculum

To help students with their educational planning, the dormitory counselor will need to be familiar with the offer-ings of the college curriculum, the general content of the courses, and the requirements for a major and for graduation. In talking with a girl about her work, the counselor will have opportunities to draw on this knowledge. For example, if she is familiar with the general nature of the courses Jean is tak-ing, as well as with the girl's abilities, she will be better able to understand her difficulties. Though she may not know enough about all the phases of the subject matter under discus-sion to be able to help the girl much in her thinking about it, her general familiarity with its content may give Jean a feel-ing of security. Such books as *What College Offers* (28) and *Roads to Knowledge* (34) are useful in developing an ac-quaintance with unfamiliar subject matter fields. Thus, in discussing with Mary the courses she is considering for next semester, the counselor, who knows Mary's tendency to choose the easiest, can try to interest her in other courses which might help her to awake intellectually. Again, a student may feel free to be more frank with the dormitory counselor in thinking out loud her reasons for choosing certain courses in preference to others, than she would with a faculty adviser outside the dormitory. Thus she may more readily see that her criteria are immature, and come to decide more maturely. Sometimes a girl will wish to discuss her choice of a major with the dormitory counselor. If the latter knows the required courses and prerequisites, or can quickly refresh her memory by turning to the catalogue, she will be better able to judge the suitability of the proposed major. This does not mean, necessarily, that the counselor will advise her not to major in economics because it will involve a mastery of statistical theory, which she, with her blind spot for mathematics, will find an almost impossible hurdle. However, if the counselor knows this fact, she can more easily make sure that the girl is taking it into consideration in making her choice. This more leisurely exploration of long-term educational and vocational plans is often a helpful prelude to the student's conference with her faculty adviser.

Information about Vocations and Training

Closely related to the choice of courses and of a major is the choice of a vocation. It is true that there are some openings for graduates of liberal arts colleges for which certain personality qualifications are of chief importance; in these cases specific training, except for typing and shorthand, is of minor interest. In this class are non-professional personnel positions, public relations work, and other business and government posts which are difficult to classify from the vocational standpoint. However, even for vocations which have no strictly professional requirements, experience has sometimes shown that certain courses constitute a better background than others. And in fields such as medicine, science, psychological services, social work, home economics, teaching, statistical work, law, merchandising, and the arts, a knowledge of the necessary or appropriate courses which should be included in an undergraduate program is fairly important. Certain colleges, among them Purdue University, Smith College, the University of North Carolina, Syracuse University, and Oberlin College, have published special pamphlets for the use of students, showing how the curricular offerings are related to a wide range of vocations such as these. Such graphic presentations of this information, which not only list required and desirable courses and advanced training, but also include descriptions of the work, the present demand for it, and the types of positions available, are interesting to students and very usable.

The dormitory counselor should know not only the nature of the undergraduate and graduate training required for the common vocations, but also the best places to secure such training; she should be familiar with both standard graduate schools and highly specialized training schools, such as the Rhode Island School of Design or the Philadelphia School of Occupational Therapy. Many institutions of this latter type are affiliated with near-by colleges and offer a cooperative program leading to a professional degree. Certain professional agencies such as the American Medical Association, the National League of Nursing Education, the American Association of Social Workers, the American Dietetic Association, and certain government bureaus, especially the U. S. Office of Education, supply full information about accredited institutions for training. Such a compendium of information as *A Guide to Colleges, Universities, and Professional Schools* (12) would be extremely useful in the Residence Halls Office. Decision as to the best place to secure the given training must be made with reference to the girl's ability and financial resources and the suitability of its location for her, as well as to its professional standing. As Strang (46) suggested, it is helpful to keep on file charts or lists of the best training schools

for each vocational field. Since many students find that investigation of the nature of the required training through the
catalogue descriptions of courses helps them to decide whether
a vocation is suitable, there is justification for giving some
emphasis to catalogue study as one aspect of vocational guidance.

The dormitory counselor needs a general knowledge of the
nature of the work, the qualifications, the opportunities for
advancement, and the present demand in the major vocations,
or at least she needs the ability to refer the student to available sources of information. The monographs called *Careers* [11]
supply up-to-date information. A complete set of these should
be in the college library. *Women's Work and Education* [12]
is a quarterly which furnishes excellent current material and
also reviews new publications on vocations. The most complete index to all the current literature on vocations is the
Occupational Index (35).

Since one of the best ways of determining the appropriateness of a vocation is to have a trial job in the field during a
vacation, the dormitory counselor should know what kinds of
part-time positions are available to undergraduates and how
to get them. In many cases, the student can be referred to the
Placement Office for this kind of help. It is well for the counselor to know, also, the local resources: institutions to visit, or
successful persons in the various vocational fields who are willing to be interviewed by students. She might invite these
persons to have dinner at the dormitory with groups of students who desire information about their occupations.

Thus, if adequate specialized vocational guidance service is
not available to all the students, the dormitory counselor must
be a source of information. However, she will always make
use of the student's ingenuity in getting information for herself. She will first find out what the student already knows

[11] Published by the Institute for Research, Chicago, Ill.
[12] Published by the Institute of Women's Professional Relations, New
London, Conn.

about a given field, then get her to see what more she needs to know. To check the strength of reported interests, she may give the student one or more of the vocational interest tests referred to above. She will also need to assist the girl to appraise her abilities for a particular vocation, making use of test results and her own observations, as well as reports of performance on summer jobs.

Knowledge of Effective Study Techniques

Some students need help in the improvement of their study habits; they lack understanding of their study potentialities. In the past they have simply been advised to study harder or to spend more time on their work. They are surprised to learn that there are so many tricks of the trade and regret that they did not know about them before.

The dormitory counselor should have at hand for student use such study guides as the Birds' *Learning More by Effective Study* (4) or Wrenn and Larson's *Studying Effectively* (59). Cole's *Background for College Teaching* (7) will help the counselor appreciate the special difficulties some students have with certain college subjects. No formula can or should be prescribed to a student in difficulty, since each one has to work out her best plan of attack. What the student must do is to analyze her present habits of study and reading to find out what is wrong. In so doing, she may ask herself questions such as these:

1. Do I begin to work at once, instead of dawdling? Do I determine to read with an active attitude?

2. Do I try to ascertain the purpose of the assignment and get a preliminary view of its scope? Do I understand what I am supposed to get from it, and in this light determine where I should put most stress?

3. Do I review the notes of the previous lecture and try to see how they relate to the present assignment?

4. If it is a reading assignment, do I first examine chapter,

section, and paragraph headings to get an idea of its organization?

5. As I read do I keep in mind the questions suggested by
this cursory examination?

6. Do I vary my rate of reading, depending on the type
of material and its relative importance?

7. Do I read with the *intent* of remembering the main
points?

8. After reading a chapter, or a section of a very long
chapter, do I give an oral summary of it or recite its main
points to myself, afterwards checking my accuracy of recall?

9. Is my outlining more than a mechanical process of
copying paragraph headings? Do I read to comprehend and
then take notes trying to use my own words in the phrasing
of the topics?

10. As I read, do I compare what I already know about the
subject with the new ideas presented?

11. As I read, do I mentally note the organization of each
paragraph and see how one paragraph leads logically to the
next, paying special attention to transition words and phrases?

12. When I take notes, do I make them legible and organize
them so well that I can see at a glance the structure of a chapter? Do I make a practice of reading the material over before
starting to take notes? In class, do I try to get the pattern of
the lecturer's thought before starting to take notes?

13. Do I review every week or so, instead of leaving it all
until the examination?

14. If there are deficiencies in my background, especially
in languages, mathematics, and science, do I take the initiative
in eliminating them as soon as possible? Do I constantly drill
myself on my weak points?

15. When I get bored, do I insist on working until I have
my second wind?

16. If it is a course in which the examinations contain questions of the essay type, do I give myself practice by composing
good questions and making myself write out the answers in

a limited period of time, always checking them for accuracy and careful organization?

Lists of such questions may be mimeographed for use with students. Most college students, once they have located their difficulty, are capable of taking remedial measures themselves. The counselor must always encourage a student to use her own resources in locating and solving her problems.

Sometimes a student expresses a desire for help in using the library effectively, in making an outline, or in writing a research paper. The counselor may refer her to the librarian, to her English instructor, or to a book such as *You and College* (27).

If a girl's principal difficulty is poor time-planning, the counselor may suggest that she keep an accurate twenty-four-hour schedule for a week, so that she herself, as well as the counselor, may see how she actually does spend her time. Sometimes it is a revelation to a girl to find out how much time she fritters away. The student can then decide what changes and adjustments she ought to make in order to get everything in. Unfortunately, college assignments vary so enormously and there are so many unpredictable meetings and other events that it is not possible for a girl to stick to a schedule in which every hour of the day is planned. However, most students have trouble because they procrastinate on long-term assignments.

The Improvement of Reading

Whether the dormitory counselor is responsible for diagnosis and remediation of reading deficiencies depends, of course, on whether there is on the campus a reading clinic or a personnel worker trained in this function. One cannot prescribe a formula for the process of diagnosis because of the many variables which enter into it, such as the amount of time available, the counselor's training, and the nature of the difficulty. Assuming that the counselor has discovered a student's reading deficiency from the school record or through an interview with the student, her first step is to check with the college doctor to be sure there is no visual defect. She may then give an appropriate reading test, together with an informal oral test using passages from one of the student's texts. The oral reading is useful in detecting difficulty with word recognition or sentence structure, and in revealing the student's method of attacking unfamiliar words and comprehending the passage as a whole. The counselor will also want to find out about the girl's leisure reading habits and tastes. The writer has found that many freshmen who are deficient in reading do almost no voluntary reading; thus their difficulty moves in a vicious circle, since they get little practice to increase their fluency in reading.

The remedial measures to be taken will depend on the amount of time the girl is able to devote to the problem and the strength of her determination to overcome the deficiency, as well as on the nature of the difficulty. For example, if her basic vocabulary and comprehension skills are good and she needs merely to speed up her reading, it often helps to practice timing herself on the reading required in her courses and training herself to look sharply at the paragraph pattern, the key words, and the transitional words. However, the girl's lack of time is a very real problem in all remedial reading work. Her low reading ability causes her to spend an inordinately long time on assignments. It may be impossible for her to put in an extra half hour or more daily without some readjustment of her program. Self-help exercise books which the student will find helpful are Strang's *Study Type of Reading Exercises* (48) and Triggs' manual, *Improve Your Reading* (84). *Problems in the Improvement of Reading* (29) is an excellent book for the counselor to study, whether she has had training in remedial reading or not.

Diagnosis

A student who has persistent study and reading difficulties may be a subject for special study. The dormitory counselor may ask herself: How did Jane get into this state of abject hopelessness about her work? What is her school and personal history to date? What kinds of abilities does she have and what are her chief interests? What past or present causes of conflict are absorbing the energy which should be going into a constructive attack on her problem? What attitude do her parents have toward her education? Could there be a physical cause? Have her eyes been checked? What are her study and reading habits? Is a thorough diagnosis of her reading difficulties in order? What is her underlying personality structure? With such a student, the counselor will never look at academic deficiencies in isolation. She will attempt to answer questions such as the above by studying the cumulative record, by interviewing the girl, and by using tests, study habit inventories, or time schedules. For a girl who finds talking difficult, autobiographies or questionnaires may be especially helpful. In any case, it is important to determine the best way of working with the girl as well as the reasons for her lack of adjustment. Sometimes, even when the dormitory counselor recognizes that the real cause is a deeper one, she will decide to try to help her with immediate surface problems of study habits. At other times, as Heaton (17) pointed out, attention to habits and skills may be ineffectual when emotions or health are the real core of the problem.

The dormitory counselor who possesses good judgment and psychological insight and who has known a girl over a period of time will be in a good position to make a tentative diagnosis with the help of the college physician, psychiatrist, or other specialist. A counselor recently called the attention of the head of residence to a certain girl who, she felt, had been acting unnaturally. The previous year she had been enthusiastic, alive, glowing; now she seemed to be depressed and unhappy and eager to avoid meeting people. The head of residence had not been aware of this change in behavior because she had not been there the year before to know the girl in her normal state. Actually, the student was suffering from a serious depression, and she was referred to a skilled psychiatrist. Her recovery in a few months was gratifying.

REFERRAL PROCEDURES

Referral to a Psychiatrist

A head of residence or dormitory counselor occasionally needs to refer a girl to someone with specialized knowledge or skill. Especially when she recognizes in a girl any of the danger signals referred to in the last chapter, she can help best by trying to interpret to the girl the kind of services a psychiatrist can render. If there is no psychiatrist on the college staff, the question of expense arises. The counselor needs to know whether the college bears any part of that expense and approximately what the cost to the family will be. Whether the family is to pay for the service or not, someone in authority in the college must secure the permission of the parents if anything more than an exploratory interview is to be held. This aspect of referral takes patience and tact. Unfortunately, few families can accept the possibility of mental illness in the same way they accept physical illness. Though some other administrative officer of the college, usually the college physician, may make the contact both with the family and with the psychiatrist, the head of residence or residence counselor must know the proper channels through which to work. The counselor's chief duties will be to maintain a supporting relationship with the girl and to report her own observations to the persons who need this information.

The following illustration may make clearer the part played by the dormitory counselor. Grace was a brilliant girl with an excellent academic record. She had been expressing feelings of utter worthlessness for which there seemed to be no basis. This condition got steadily worse until the girl seemed unable to make any decisions for herself. The counselor, after discussing Grace's symptoms and unhappy home situation with the Dean of Residence, explained to the girl that it was possible for her to understand herself better and to make a happier adjustment in college by talking to a doctor who would know how to help her. At first Grace felt that she could not possibly talk to a person she did not know. Then she said that if the counselor would tell the psychiatrist all about her, and if he seemed to understand her, perhaps she would consent to see him. She was very insistent that her family must not know. When she mentioned the subject of the expense, the counselor explained that the college would pay for the first interview and diagnosis and that her family would not need to be consulted about that. After that, she could decide whether to go ahead. Thus reassured, the girl said that she would be willing for the dormitory counselor to make an appointment for her, through the Dean of Residence. The counselor suggested to the dean that a psychiatrist having a religious approach would probably be able to do the most for Grace. Meanwhile, the counselor made sure that one of Grace's friends was always with her. The counselor accompanied her to the psychiatrist, introduced her, and left. One of Grace's friends brought her home. The psychiatrist later phoned the Dean to say that he thought it was probably safe for her to stay in the dormitory during the treatment and that she had responded favorably to the idea of coming for a series of interviews. This information the Dean at once communicated to the counselor, who then had the difficult task of explaining to the girl that it would be necessary to inform her parents of the situation and to get their consent for the treatment. Grace was upset, but finally agreed to their being told. The Dean telephoned the parents, who at first expressed the opinion that Grace had made up this story in order to get sympathy. However, the Dean was able to get them to see the psychiatrist, who sometimes made trips to their city. They agreed reluctantly to allow the treatment, and promised not to visit the daughter until she was better. During the therapy, which lasted some months, the counselor saw the girl constantly and made frequent reports to the Dean; she also wrote to the parents. The psychiatrist described to the counselor the kind of help both she and Grace's friends could render. The latter, after an interview with the counselor, were untiring in their efforts to draw the girl gradually into normal activities. This girl's cure was accomplished slowly. If she had not had confidence in the dormitory counselor, the referral would have been much more difficult. Thus, the counselor was a key person in the curative process.

Referral to Other Experts

A much more common type of referral occurs when a student needs some sort of specialized information or help which the dormitory counselor does not feel competent to give. For example, she may suggest that a girl go to a social agency to get information about openings in the field of social work and about opportunities for volunteer work in the summer as tryout experience. She may send another girl to the physical education department for advice on reducing exercises. In most cases of this sort, it is better for the student herself to take the initiative in making the appointment.

If the girl needs help of a more personal nature, the counselor should give the new consultant some information about her. Sometimes she will be able to do this openly, after discussing with the student what she would like the other person to know about her. For example, one girl was referred to a speech instructor. Her stuttering had made her extremely shy in talking with strangers, though she rarely stuttered in the presence of someone with whom she felt at ease. She had recently dropped the course she had been taking with the speech teacher, Miss Benson. The interview was as follows:

COUNSELOR. You think it would be easier if I were to talk to Miss Benson about you?
STUDENT. Yes, I'd appreciate it a lot if you would. I think that way she might be more interested in helping me. You know, it's sort of hard for me to talk about myself, and especially with her because she doesn't know why I dropped her course.

COUNSELOR. I'll be glad to. Now, what do you think she ought to know about you?

STUDENT. Well, it might be good for her to know what we think started me off stuttering and how I always do w-when I talk to anybody I don't know or when a lot of people are around. Do you think of anything else?

COUNSELOR. No, except about her class.

STUDENT. Of course. Tell her we thought that if I had a little special help for a while, I might go back to her class.

The counselor should never embarrass a girl by talking about her to another person in her presence. Rather, she should discuss with the girl her feeling about referral and the help they both hope the other person will be able to give.

Resources for Referral

The head of residence must certainly know the resources for referral on the campus and in the town, and must be familiar with the means of getting in touch with these persons. There are enormous variations among colleges and communities as to the number of professional people who may be called upon. Included in this category are: the librarian, for students who need help in improving their reading habits, in making better use of the library, and in searching for vocational information; a member of the speech department who has a special interest in the personality problems of students; the chaplain, or those ministers in the town who have an interest in students; the director of the placement office; a member of the physical education department who has information about the social and recreational needs of some of the students, or who can give individual help in the acquisition of such skills as dancing or tennis; and other more obvious resources such as class deans, the social director, the college doctor, and the psychiatrist. Because of the nature of their work, too, members of the art, drama, and music departments are often especially good sources of information about individual students; because of their close contact with students, they can often be very helpful counselors.

INTERVIEWING THEORY AND PROCEDURES

The knowledge and techniques described in this chapter and the last form a useful background for the dormitory counselor in her direct contacts with individual students in the residence hall. These contacts cover a wide range, from a casual greeting to a long series of interviews; and each of them, however brief, has potentialities for student development. If she understands the theory and procedures of interviewing, she will be able to realize more fully the potential values of the many interviews which she holds in the residence hall.

Impossibility of Classifying Dormitory Interviews

Authorities have attempted to classify interviews according to their purposes: for example, fact-finding, employment, health, vocational, personality adjustment, admission to college, educational guidance, discipline, and referral. For interviews with students, especially in the dormitory, these classifications are somewhat artificial. To be sure, the dormitory counselor sometimes calls a student in for the special purpose of getting some information about her. At the same time, however, she will probably open up areas for subsequent discussion. As a result of the counselor's friendly interest, the student's attitude toward the college may become more favorable and her behavior may change. The following interview illustrates these possibilities:

COUNSELOR. I thought you might like to talk over with me how things are going so far, any difficulties you might have had, and so on. And I wanted to get better acquainted with you. How are things going?

STUDENT. Oh, not so bad, but they could be better.

COUNSELOR. Yes? In what way?

STUDENT. I just got a paper back in English. I thought in high school that I could write—even thought I might do it for a living. So I was sort of upset by what she wrote on it.

COUNSELOR. So that discouraged you and the discouragement spread to other things.

STUDENT. Yes, I guess we do let one thing bother us too much sometimes.

COUNSELOR. Yours is a difficulty many of the freshmen have. There's often such a big difference between high school and college standards of writing. But quite a number of those who feel most discouraged turn up later writing for the college magazine.

STUDENT. Probably there are things that need working on. And it's better, maybe, to begin low and work up.

COUNSELOR. A good idea. And how do you feel about things?

STUDENT. Oh, I'm really loving some things about college, especially the girls in the dorm. You know I went to a sort of snooty prep school where there were very few girls from the other side of the railroad tracks. What I like here is that there are so many different kinds. There are two foreign girls on my corridor, from France and Greece, and they have made me realize how provincial and smug some of us are.

COUNSELOR. If you want to write, you have one excellent qualification: your interest in all kinds of people and ability to draw them out.

STUDENT. Yes, I love to talk to people. In fact, it may be my downfall.

COUNSELOR. Meaning?

STUDENT. I can't make myself get my work done. And how it does pile up!

Counselor. So you feel swamped at times. I suppose at school you had regular study hours.

STUDENT. Yes, I guess I mostly did things only because I had to. Here where your classes are mostly lecture, it's so easy to let things go. I should make a schedule and make myself stick to it.

COUNSELOR. Would you like to try accounting for your time for a week and then have us look over your schedule together to see how much time you can really afford to spend that way?

STUDENT. Yes, I think that might give me a jolt. I'll start tomorrow. Shall I come in at the same time next week?

This interview could scarcely be classified simply as fact-finding. The counselor got some useful information about the girl's personality and recent adjustment, but the interview, brief as it was, also gave the student an opportunity to express to a discerning person her feelings about various aspects of college life, and to gain a little self-understanding.

Principles of Interviewing

Student's capacity for self-direction.—Of the several principles which are basic to interviewing, faith in the student's capacity for self-direction is the most important. The residence hall counselor must think of the student as a free and responsible agent with the ability, in most cases, to work out her own problems; the counselor must respect her as a relatively mature person. By displaying an overanxious attitude or too great an eagerness to help, the counselor may imply that she lacks confidence in the student. However, allowing her to "work out her own problems" does not mean withholding support and help. Definite suggestions are sometimes in order when a girl is so upset that she is incapable of making an important decision. There are also a few instances in which advice must be given in order to prevent a girl from following a course which would be disastrous. When the counselor is really in a better position to judge the wisdom of various alternatives, her point of view is one source of information for the student. At its best counseling helps a girl to become progressively more independent, better able to solve her problems by the use of her own resources, as in the following example.

Dorothy was upset about her seeming inability to decide on a suitable vocation. She thought tests would give her the answer and was disappointed that they only opened further areas for exploration. Then she looked to the counselor to tell her the solution: "What do *you* think I am best fitted for and what do you think I ought to do?" The counselor asked her what she felt her strong and weak points were and discussed the data on the cumulative record with her. She gave Dorothy the results of the Strong and the Kuder vocational interest tests and helped her to interpret these in the light of what she already knew about herself. The counselor then asked her what experiences she had had which might help her to choose, and discussed with her the summer jobs she had held. When Dorothy seemed able to focus her interest on two vocations as having greatest appeal, the counselor encouraged her to explore them by the use of the library and other sources of information. Eventually, Dorothy was able to pool her knowledge about herself and the vocations and come to an independent decision. There were three interviews with the counselor. Had the dependent attitude Dorothy displayed at the beginning been associated with emotional deprivation, the counselor would have needed more time and skill in guiding her to take the initiative.

It is sad but true that some counselors get satisfaction from the feeling that someone is dependent on them, and thus have a sort of vested interest in perpetuating this kind of relationship. This type of counselor must find other ways to satisfy her managerial drives. She must try to curb the feeling that something *has* to be done about this student and that she alone can do it. She must not impose her solution, but must rather say to the student: "What I would do in your case is perhaps not the point. Let's see if we can figure out what you really need to do and what will be most satisfactory to you in the end." The counselor who has worked in an academic office or has taught is peculiarly susceptible to the temptation to give the student academic "prescriptions" and to do too much of the talking. Questions such as, "Had you thought of the possibility of doing that?" or "What would you think of doing this?" put more responsibility on the girl. If the counselor takes too much responsibility for decisions which the student is able to make herself, or if she tries to do the girl's thinking for her, she is robbing her of the chance to become a more mature person. Advising and persuading may appear to get results quickly, especially with rather dependent girls, but they do not accomplish as much in the long run. Occasionally there will be emergency situations in which quick action must be taken by someone in authority. Sometimes, too, there is a place for advice. But, as Garrett (11) said, one trouble with advice is that the counselor does not know enough about the girl's capacity to carry it out; she bases it on her own experience. The counselor's function is rather to give the girl the information (or tell her where to get it) on which the decision must be based, and to create a secure emotional atmosphere in which she can figure out the solution for herself. When the counselor does give advice, she should assure the girl that she does not need to accept it and that the counselor's willingness to help her is in no way dependent on whether she carries out the suggestions.

Some authorities on counseling think that to give a student information instead of allowing her to look it up herself is to make her dependent. Possibly there is this danger. It is also true that the way a girl goes after information is a real test of how much she wants it. However, if the counselor has information at hand which it would be rather difficult for the girl to get, and especially if it would take the time of others to help her, then it is more practical for the counselor to give her the information, provided she is sure that the girl is ready for it. Unfortunately, suggestions and information are often given gratuitously by a dean or counselor who wants to feel that she is "doing something."

Role of the dormitory counselor as co-worker and catalytic agent.—While the responsibility for making decisions rests with the student, counseling is a cooperative undertaking in which counselor and student work together to see what plans can be evolved to meet a situation. The counselor does not conceive a plan which she feels is best for the student and then subtly try to guide her thinking toward it. She does not know at the outset what solution would be best, since part of her job is to try to see the situation through the student's eyes. True, she may add something to the girl's thinking to make sure that the latter considers all sides of a question. But in general the counselor tries to facilitate the student's thinking. As finally worked out, the solution or decision is the girl's, though the counselor has contributed toward it.

In accepting the student's expressed feelings the counselor also acts as a catalytic agent. Acceptance means, not a condoning of the girl's behavior or a negative refusal to pass judgment, but a positive effort to understand the girl and her feelings, no matter how unsocial.

Her need for sympathetic objectivity.—A dormitory counselor must strive to maintain an attitude of benevolent objectivity or professional friendliness, and must avoid cultivating a more intense emotional relationship. If she can maintain that objective attitude, she will not take personally the hostility which a girl will occasionally show. She will understand that it is probably not directed toward her individually, but may be a substitute for hostility toward a parent or sibling. Of course, she will examine her relations with the student to be sure that her own behavior has not been at fault. Neither will she be flattered or disturbed by the unusual attentions of the student who gets a "crush" on her. She will not allow herself to become emotionally involved in a girl's difficulties, but, at the same time, she will try not to appear impersonal or unsympathetic. Too great objectivity may appear to some students to be rejection.

Her need for recognition of prejudices.—The counselor needs to examine herself for prejudices. Perhaps, for example, loud, raucous laughter, a dirty, unkempt appearance, or the tendency to play to the gallery may annoy her excessively. On the other hand, a cheerful manner and pleasant smile, or an engaging habit of confiding in the counselor or of expressing gratitude to her, may play too important a role in the counselor's analysis of a girl. It is not humanly possible, of course, to feel the same toward all dormitory students. However, the counselor must try not to identify herself strongly with certain students, nor can she allow prejudices against the behavior of others to color her judgment. She may ask herself: "Does this girl repel me so that I cannot like her?" "Is it hard for me to see rudeness without becoming angry?" "Do I tend to respond so favorably to this type of girl that I am kept from understanding her fully?" Probably the dormitory counselor cannot help some of her prejudices. However, she can be aware of them and take them into account. If she finds that they block her ability to help certain girls, she should try to refer these girls to another counselor.

Her triple role as person in authority, friend, and profes-sional helper.—The role of the counselor in the dormitory is sometimes complicated by the fact that her administrative duties cause her to be associated in some girls' minds with an idea of discipline that is contrary to the principles of personnel work. Whether that is a handicap depends on how success-fully she can demonstrate the idea that a student who needs discipline is, as Hawkes (14) put it, a student in trouble, whose motives need understanding. If the counselor is able to show the student that she really understands her unsocial attitudes and conduct, even while she is passing judgment on them, and that she is genuinely interested in her as a person, she will probably be able to help her. She must have faith in the girl's potentialities and assets, but at the same time she must not gloss over her faults. For example, a certain rather immature freshman whose head had been turned by attention from the near-by university boys had been brought to the counselor by the night watchman, who reported that she and a boy friend had been found in the basement where it was rather dark. The counselor asked the girl to come to talk to her the next morn-ing, since, as she said, the girl would probably not be able to discuss the incident objectively at the moment. Meanwhile, she had to explain to the night watchman, who appeared shocked, that she had not administered summary punishment, and why she was handling the matter in this way. In the inter-view which followed, the girl was at first on the defensive; however, as she became aware that the counselor was not try-ing to "put her on the spot," she began to talk freely. The counselor learned a great deal about her overstrict upbringing, and the girl began to see that her too free conduct had been a means of hitting back at former restrictions. When the counselor asked her what she really felt about the appropriateness of such behavior for herself personally, as well as about its effect on others, the girl was quite honest in condemning it.

In this case, the counselor was successful in achieving the real end product of discipline: self-control and responsible conduct on the part of the student. At the same time, the student gained a better understanding of herself. If she should need constructive help again, she would feel free to go to this counselor for it. Thus the counselor was able to avoid the possible conflict between "person in authority" and "friendly counselor."

The other potential conflict between the counselor's roles might occur in the case of a student who has a serious emotional problem and needs intensive interviewing. The counselor will have to temper her usual informal friendliness, ordinarily so desirable in the dormitory, with a still warm but more professional attitude. This transition may be difficult for the student to accept. For example, a girl who has been in the habit of dropping into the counselor's room for informal chats may find it hard to adjust to the definite time limits of regular interviews.

Should interviews always be voluntary?—Interviews are usually more effective when they are voluntary, since the student who approaches the counselor with a conscious need for assistance is already in a receptive frame of mind. However, if the counseling program is new, students may not realize the resources at their disposal or the kind of help which they may expect to receive. The head of residence may explain these resources to the students at a house meeting early in the year. Establishing a reputation for constructive personal contacts takes time, especially in a very large dormitory; it should not be expected that many students will avail themselves of the opportunity at first. Moreover, there are always some students who would never take the initiative unless they were in serious difficulty and a few others who feel that seeking help from an adult is a sign of weakness. One way of trying to reach students at the beginning is for the counselor to invite each one in for a sort of get-acquainted interview in which the student has an opportunity to talk about herself, her plans, her interests, any significant experiences she has had, the things she hopes to get from college, and the hindrances which are preventing her from making the most of these opportunities. During this interview, the dormitory counselor will have an excellent opportunity to make observations about the student. The counselor will allow her to talk freely, with a minimum of interrogating, so that she may note what things the girl chooses to talk about. The counselor may want certain information for the personnel record blank, but she should not let this be apparent, nor should she have a prepared list of questions to be covered. If the counselor does not probe, and seems easy to talk to, such an interview will open the way for further counseling.

The basic principles of interviewing may be summed up as follows:

1. The counselor must always utilize the student's own resources for helping herself, and must avoid making her dependent by too much advice and suggestion.

2. At the same time, her purpose should not be to maintain a "hands off" attitude, but rather to work with the student in finding the best solution to her problem.

3. She must learn how to accept and understand a student's feelings without approving unsocial conduct she may have shown.

4. She must learn to avoid both emotional involvement in a girl's problem and complete aloofness from it.

5. She must be aware of, and make allowances for, her prejudices toward certain individuals or characteristics, whether favorable or unfavorable.

6. Her discipline, in the best sense of the word, must be constructive and in accord with the personnel point of view; thus she can be both an efficient administrator and a friendly counselor.

7. Interviews, especially in the early stages of a counseling program, cannot always be voluntary. However, the exploratory type of interview, even though requested, may be very helpful in building up the students' feeling of confidence in the counselor.

The Process of Interviewing

The discussion which follows has to do with the more formal contacts. The fact that so much space is given to them does not mean that casual conversations in the dormitory are not also valuable in aiding the growth of students. Chapter Two made extensive references to the informal contact, and explored its potentialities to some degree. Since planned interviews require more skill if they are to be fruitful, it is worth while to discuss them in some detail.

Setting for interviews.—Privacy and a minimum of interruptions are important. True, certain kinds of interviews can be conducted in the busy office of the residence hall, but such an environment is usually not conducive to free conversation. The counselor's comfortable and attractive private living room invites the necessary relaxation without hindering rigorous thinking. Sometimes, the books, curios, and pictures in the room provide a means for discovering a common interest with a girl who has previously been hard to reach. The counselor should try to give the appearance of being at leisure, of having nothing on her mind at the moment but her genuine interest in the student's effort to understand herself. An atmosphere of hurry does not invite confidences. Some counselors find that by taking up some domestic activity such as knitting or sewing they can help the student to feel at home. On the other hand, a special interviewing office has a better effect on some students, perhaps because it reassures them that they are going to receive professional help.

Preparation for the interview.—First of all, it is necessary to schedule a period of sufficient length. Even students with very minor matters to discuss appreciate a special appoint-

ment; it gives them confidence that their problem will receive
due consideration. There should also be a definite time limit,
usually not more than an hour. Taft (50) and others felt that
there is a therapeutic value in setting time limits which cannot
be overstepped and within which the counselee has the responsibility to accomplish as much as possible.

Before the interview, the counselor will review pertinent
facts about the girl, and read over the content of any previous
interviews. If the counselor remembers some things about a
girl without referring to the personnel record in her presence,
the student feels that the counselor's interest is genuine. This
ability to remember is especially desirable in interviews with a
student who suspects that her personnel record is in some way
unfavorable. If the counselor anticipates the existence of a
serious personal problem, even though the student has asked
to talk of a more superficial matter, she will review what she
knows about the girl with this in mind. If she knows that the
student wants to discuss vocational plans, she will have on
hand sources of information which she can offer when the
student is ready for them. In all interviews, she will have in
mind tentative goals, but she will never allow them to govern
the course of the interview.

Since, as Strang (46) said, every interview is both unique
and complex, since the methods of approach that are effective
in one case may not get the same results in other cases, and
since each counselor must find her own best way of approaching students and working with them, it is difficult for anyone
to help the counselor improve her interviewing procedure.
Though no one can give formulas, the writer believes that
there is value in analyzing the interview, pointing out certain
procedures which have seemed desirable, and warning against
others which should be avoided.

Gaining rapport.—Good rapport is a *sine qua non* of any
interview. Snyder (42) described rapport as a kind of projection of oneself into the feelings of the counselee. A warm,
accepting manner on the part of the counselor, a sensitivity

to what the girl is thinking and feeling, usually establishes rapport and is more important than anything that is said. As Lloyd-Jones (25) said, the interview is more than a "structure of words." The interview involves the impact which two personalities make upon each other, operating in part through the medium of tone or inflection of voice, through posture, gestures, facial expression, and through the perceived attitudes and feelings of both. A natural, tension-free quality of voice is especially important. Some people think that one is either naturally equipped for this sort of relationship, or cannot do it at all. It is true that some are able to gain rapport more quickly than others. However, given intelligence and a genuine interest in people, one can acquire some skill in establishing contact with students. Perhaps a counselor will always have a few people with whom she can never "get to first base," but this may be because of such intangibles as the counselor's resemblance to someone the student has previously disliked. Moreover, rapport is not gained once and for all. It maybe lost through a tactless question or premature advice.

Initial structuring of the interview.—It is often desirable in the first interview for the counselor to tell the student something of what she may get from the counseling experience, especially if she has a complicated problem requiring more than one interview. The first contact might proceed something like this:

COUNSELOR. You said you felt confused and thought you wanted to get some help in thinking through your plans for the future—what to prepare for here at college.

STUDENT. Yes, that's what I want. I thought you might be able to tell me what I was best fitted for. And maybe I could take some tests, too.

COUNSELOR. Well, I think I ought to explain the kind of help you might be able to get. By telling me about yourself, your interests, likes, and dislikes, any past experiences that you think might have any bearing on the present, and what your thinking has been to date on this business of choosing a vocation, you can help us both see more clearly what you are like and what you

really want. Then, if you like, you may take one or more tests
that are supposed to clarify your interests, and we can check on
your general ability. There are no very satisfactory tests that
measure ability for a specific vocation, for most vocations that
college students follow are too complex. Anyway, the way you
feel about certain kinds of work, the previous experiences you
have had, the satisfactions you've got from your part-time work
are more important. Then you will need to do some research on
the fields of work you think you would like best for yourself.
We shall have to do quite a lot of thinking to see whether what
you know about yourself would fit into the requirements of a
vocation and whether it is a practical one for you. All this will
give you a basis for your decision which no one but you can make.
Does this seem a reasonable way of approaching the thing?

STUDENT. Yes, I think it does. I guess I just didn't realize that
it would involve so much. I guess I just wanted to be told.

COUNSELOR. Does it seem like too much work to you? Do you
want to try to work it out that way?

STUDENT. It's bothered me quite a lot and is really very important to me. So, if you have the time, I'd like to. Could I make
an appointment for tomorrow?

Here the counselor has helped the student to state her problem
more clearly and has structured the situation; that is, she has
defined the limits within which they may work.

If the counselor suspects that the request for vocational
guidance is a disguised request for help with deep-seated personality problems (vocational guidance being a "respectable"
area to begin on until one has sounded out the counselor a
little), then by defining the procedure in this way she may
have made the mistake of blocking the path to the real problem. Especially if the girl is inclined to be dependent (and she
has revealed this by saying, "I thought you might be able to
tell me"), she may feel that she had better carry out the plan
exactly as described. She may not even be aware that this is
not her real problem. In such a case, the counselor might
better have said at the beginning, "Probably you know yourself pretty well. Suppose you tell me what your thinking has
been on this problem." That would have set the stage for an
exploratory type of interview in the course of which the girl

might have discovered that her real difficulty is inability to make a decision, and that it rises from lack of self-confidence. However, even if the counselor has started out with the first type of structuring, she may still encourage the girl to explore every aspect of her problem.

The art of listening.—Listening is an important part of the counselor's activity during an interview. The word *activity* is here used advisedly, since her listening is by no means a passive process. She is busy observing cues and wondering what they mean. For example, the girl is doing a lot of fidgeting during the interview, and does not look the counselor in the eye. Is she twisting the lamp chain and biting her nails because she feels ill at ease with the counselor, or does her embarrassment come from a feeling of guilt of some kind? She talks a great deal about her family's accomplishments. Is that to cover up her own feeling of inadequacy, or to enhance herself? Is this excessive volubility an attempt to set up a barrier of small talk which may obscure her real problem? Why is she asking for information—is it a normal request or is it to test the counselor? A rather lonely girl who feels herself rejected by her parents and has not made a very good social adjustment may talk at great length about the cottage her father made for her in the woods and of her delight in furnishing it. What does all that mean to her? Superficially, it might indicate an interest in interior decoration. But more important is its meaning as a bridge to her father: he made the house for *her*. Her delight in furnishing the place may also be a means of bolstering a weak ego; she identifies herself with the house. This is not to suggest that nothing the student says should be taken at face value. But where the counselor knows that the student is emotionally disturbed, she is alert to the deeper significances that attitudes may have.

That is why it is important not to be so much concerned with the machinery of the interview that one cannot concentrate on what the student is thinking and feeling. The counselor needs to function on two levels, as it were: (1) to note

the objective facts in what the student is saying; and (2) to
be alert to the evident attitudes, feelings, and tensions that are
concealed behind what the girl is saying. This is a skill learned
by experience, though perhaps never completely learned.

The use of pauses.—The inexperienced counselor may tend
to think only of what the girl says. Or she may have her mind
on the next question, or be worrying because she feels that
she ought to be able to say something to help the girl—and
cannot decide what she should say. Doubtless the pauses
which occur will seem awkward to her and she will feel im-
pelled to say something, anything, to break the silence. She
must remember, however, that this is not a social conversation
and that the pauses may be important in giving the girl time to
think or in indicating an emotional block on her part. In the
latter case, the counselor needs to help by asking the sort of
question that will make it easy for her to go on; for example,
referring to something significant that was said previously, or
encouraging her to think of other aspects of the problem. The
counselor also needs to adjust her pace to that of the girl; she
must not hurry her. Sometimes it is a good idea to appear to be
in a meditative mood oneself. However, while the counselor
needs to hold herself in check lest she talk too much and thus
hinder the student from talking spontaneously, she should
avoid the other extreme—complete silence—which might
suggest lack of interest or make the girl feel that she is not
understood.

*The art of responding to the student's feelings and to the
meaning underlying her words.*—If an emotional problem
exists, the student should have an opportunity to express whatever feelings are uppermost. It should not be necessary for
the counselor to tell her that she may say what she likes; the
counselor's manner should be genuinely accepting. The student's feelings will probably be negative, showing hostility
toward some person or utter discouragement with herself. For
example, the girl may say, "I just never can please her. She
seems to take pleasure in picking on me." The counselor will

merely comment in a neutral manner, "That bothers you quite a lot, doesn't it?" Here she is responding to the feeling of resentment the girl expressed, not to the words she said. One can reassure a girl that her feelings or behavior are understood without implying that they are commendable. If the counselor protests, instead, that she is sure the person is not "picking on" her and that the girl needs to change her attitude, this will probably have little effect except to increase her resentment, even though for politeness' sake she may assent. Of course, the student will need to change her attitude toward people, but this change will not come about by argument or persuasion. Some people will object that we are advising the counselor merely to encourage the girl to project blame or pity herself. This result does not necessarily follow, because when the individual has relieved her negative feelings, she will be more free to look at her situation with a new perspective. She will no longer need to be on the defensive. Feeling herself understood, she will be better able to accept her weaknesses in the light of a new and hopeful view of herself. If she is going to "blow up" anyway, it is better that she do it to a counselor who will try to make constructive use of her expression of feelings, rather than to her roommate who will either scold or encourage her.

Emotional catharsis is more of a relief and easier to handle if it is concerned with a recent event. For example, if a girl has had a terrifying experience, it is wise for her to talk about it at once, rather than to repress the memory. On the other hand, where there are hostile or guilty feelings that have long been buried, feelings connected with something which happened long ago, it may be best for an inexperienced counselor to let sleeping dogs lie. If a girl reveals deep-seated hostile feelings accompanied by guilt, the counselor must be careful that she does not encourage her to say something that she later regrets having said. If the counselor has entertained similar feelings herself that she has never been able to express, she must not make the mistake of identifying herself with the girl and thus encouraging her, for example, to oppose her family. An attitude of benevolent neutrality is always best. If the girl feels that she has gone too far in her expression of emotions, she may show resistance by refusing to talk further or even by breaking off the contacts altogether. If this happens, it is well for the counselor to show that she understands this feeling. She might say, "You are sorry you told me all this. Probably you *resent* my knowing."

There is one kind of situation in which the dormitory counselor should not let a girl go on and on in her expression of feelings; that is, in cases of acute discouragement and depression. There came to the writer's attention a very able but immature student who was doing work far below capacity because she was dissipating her energies in a dozen different directions, never getting at her studying until late at night. She had been unable to come to any decision regarding her major field in college or her future plans; in fact, she felt incapable of making any decision. She was merely drifting along. Her incessant activity was a sort of escape. She was depressed and discouraged over what she called her spinelessness, but felt incapable of taking any positive action. She was like a squirrel in a cage, going round and round, yet getting nowhere. The counselor merely reflected her feeling, thus keeping her going in a circle. Because her trouble was related to something far below the surface, she needed more skilled help than a dormitory counselor could give.

The counselor should usually avoid false reassurance. If a student is convinced that she has flunked a course and the counselor has reason to believe that this is the case, it is useless to tell her that she may be mistaken about it and that it doesn't matter anyway. It *does* matter. After she has spilled over, she may be in a better mood to face doing something about it. Glib reassurance may simply give her the feeling that the counselor does not understand the problem, or belittles it. There is, however, another kind of reassurance that is helpful: a girl who has worried about being queer or different will be helped by knowing that others are troubled by the same things that bother her.

A sense of humor always greases the machinery of human contacts and relieves tension. However, when a girl is really troubled about something, it is usually better not to try to emphasize its humorous side. Of course, she is taking herself too seriously. But while she is all tied up inside, it is impossible for her to be sufficiently objective to see the humor. Moreover, one must not be misled by the grim humor students sometimes indulge in, for laughter may be a form of desperation as well as a means of release. As a girl once said to the writer, "Perhaps I am laughing to keep myself from crying." Humorous treatment of anxieties may make a girl feel that she is not being taken seriously.

The need for helping the student to gain insight.—When a girl has the assurance that her feelings are recognized and understood, she is usually able to gain some insight into her motivations. Curran (8) says that in clarifying the girl's feelings by responding to them, even when they are inconsistent, the counselor gives her an understanding of why she acts as she does. However, she is more likely to arrive at this self-understanding if the talking out is followed by the sort of questions and comments on the counselor's part that help her to see new relationships and bring her to the point of thinking about plans. It is better for a girl to arrive at an insight herself than to have it pointed out to her. For example, a girl who talks constantly about the accomplishments of her family, avoiding any reference to her own problems of social adjustment, eventually comes to recognize that she is using this identification with her family as a compensation and as an escape from facing her own problems. The counselor should refrain from pointing this out to her, even though she may see it at the very beginning. Such an interview might proceed as follows:

COUNSELOR. It gives you great satisfaction to talk about your family. But I wonder why you do it so much.

STUDENT. I don't know—I just like to. It makes me feel sort of comfortable and good inside—[pause].

COUNSELOR. Do you want to tell me more about that? I'm trying to see what this talk of your family's accomplishments may have to do with you.

STUDENT. Well, I guess it sort of builds me up.

COUNSELOR. You mean, you don't feel so adequate yourself and if you think of yourself as a part of them, it makes you feel bigger?

STUDENT. That's it, I guess. It makes me feel important.

COUNSELOR. We all need to feel important. You think this may really help you in the long run?

STUDENT. Well, I don't know—Maybe I'm sort of using them as a shield.

COUNSELOR. Do you want to tell me more about that?

STUDENT. Well, I guess I just want to be comfortable and not face the necessity of doing something about myself.

This counselor might be criticized for rushing the girl, as when she says, "You think this may really help you in the long run?" However, in this actual case, subsequent interviews seemed to indicate that the girl's insights were genuine and that she had the capacity for acting on her knowledge.

The role of questions.—It has been said above that a student is more likely to gain self-understanding if her thinking is guided by skillful questions and comments. Such questions serve a variety of purposes. For example, a broad question at the beginning, which gives no cues as to what the counselor wants discussed, is designed to get the girl to talk freely of anything she pleases. This is better than a specific question, which, though it may yield information, may not open up important areas which need to be explored. One might say, "Tell me any experiences you have had which might have a bearing on this problem"; or, with a new student, "How have things been going with you?" Questions are frequently asked for clarification: "I don't think I quite understand what you mean by that." When a girl seems to have come to a dead end, when there is a long pause, a neutral question is often effective: "Do you think there could be other elements in the situation?"

Questions may also be asked, or comments may be made, to bring the student back to the main problem if she has gone too far afield. For example, a girl who lacks self-confidence in a social situation, owing to extreme dependence on her family, may be telling in unflattering terms what she thinks of certain news commentators. The counselor realizes that she may be doing this because it makes her feel superior or because she wishes to avoid the main problem. Of course, the counselor should not tell her this. Instead, she may say when there is a pause, "I am wondering whether you would care to tell me a little more about this fear of talking to people at social gatherings that you mentioned a while ago. In what instances have you noted it, especially?"

As the student talks, the counselor needs to be on the alert for significant points that should be taken up later for elaboration. Following is a portion of an interview with a girl whose chief problem was an inability to relate herself to others, based on a deep feeling of personal inadequacy. One problem had been solved. The more serious matter of personality adjustment had been defined, but not thoroughly faced. The counselor had been trying to get the girl to take the initiative in the interview by explaining that the time was hers to talk about whatever she wished.

COUNSELOR. You're sure that you feel you want to talk things over with me. I had the impression that you felt, now that plans for next year are settled, that there isn't so much point.

STUDENT. Yes, I really do. I think it would help—[pause].

COUNSELOR. There was something you said last time that I wondered about: you spoke of feeling "different" or "strange" when you started in on the summer job. Do you want to explain that a little?

STUDENT. I don't think I used the right word; I should have said "out of place."

COUNSELOR. You felt you didn't quite belong?

STUDENT. Yes. And I was sort of apathetic. I lived in a dream world, I guess.

Note that the counselor used one of the student's own statements, not sufficiently explored before, to bring her back to her main problem.

Questions and comments also serve the purpose of helping a person to see the connection between feelings and attitudes in one area of experience and in another. The counselor may say, "I wonder whether you see any connection between your fears in this situation and what you told me about the first time you went there alone." Here is an excerpt from an actual interview in which the counselor attempted to help the student relate one part of her experience to another:

STUDENT. I realize that for a career it's important to be able to make friends more successfully. It's not so hard to have casual relationships. But for real friendships—that's different.
COUNSELOR. Do you think there could be any connection here with previous experiences?
STUDENT. Yes. I guess I'm afraid of criticism.
COUNSELOR. You mean, that when you have been hurt in one situation you think the same thing might happen again? It's safer not to run the risk?
STUDENT. Yes, that's it. It's probably a carry-over.

One of the most difficult aspects of the art of questioning is the timing—deciding when it is best to try to help a student perceive a relationship or clarify an insight. The excerpt above might be criticized on the ground that the counselor went too fast in her effort to clarify what seemed like an insight. However, in this instance, her comments "clicked." Whether to try to hasten the student's insight—for example, whether to say to one who is overacting toward dominating parents, "Do you see what effect your saying that to them probably had?"—is a question only the individual counselor can decide as she tries to meet a situation.

There are certain "don'ts" in questioning. Questions that can be answered merely by "yes" or "no" should usually be avoided. Instead of asking, "Do you feel happy about that?" it is better to ask, "How do you feel about that?" It is obvious that the former question tends to suggest the answer. Asking more than one question at a time confuses the student. Ques-

tions such as "Didn't you feel concerned about that?" imply
a judgment, and tend to put a person on the defensive. Questions like "Did you ask the professor if he could give you a
little help on that?" are better than "Why don't you ask—?"
because the former merely suggests procedure, whereas the
latter is like a command. Questions that seem to probe are
not in order; the counselor must respect the girl's sense of
privacy.

It is poor procedure to ask an irrelevant question, one which
draws the attention away from the main problem. An inexperienced counselor may do this unconsciously when she feels
that she is in over her depth and is afraid she cannot handle
the emotional aspects of a situation. Here are three brief instances in which the counselor failed to follow a lead, but
asked, instead, an irrelevant question:

STUDENT. Maybe my lack of confidence goes back further—
I never stopped to think. But anyway, up to high school, I didn't
seem to have any trouble. I could always hold my own. I was
good in sports—always played with the boys—[pause].
COUNSELOR. You *are* good in swimming, aren't you?

Then followed a long speech about swimming. By her question, which was irrelevant to the main point of lack of self-
confidence and not belonging, the counselor deflected the discussion. It would have been better to say, "Can you tell me
more about how you felt when you entered high school?"

The second instance shows not only an irrelevant question,
but also poorly timed advice:

STUDENT. I think I got to feeling so badly because Father's Day
week end is coming and I won't have anyone to come.
COUNSELOR. Do you ever do anything with groups such as
Scouts or Children's Hospital work? Sometimes if you get interested in something outside yourself, it helps.
STUDENT. Oh, I would feel so inadequate doing anything like
that.

In the third instance the counselor's first question and her
subsequent comment were both irrelevant:

STUDENT. The professor said that I was doing so well in that history course. Then when I got my mark, I was *bitterly* disappointed [vehemently].

COUNSELOR. Did you ask him what the grade was based on?

STUDENT. Goodness, no! I would *never* speak to a professor about anything. I just *couldn't*.

COUNSELOR. But you know professors really don't bite. Once you make the plunge, you'll find it isn't so hard.

The student appeared unconvinced. In this case, the counselor should rather have reflected the student's strong feeling by remarking, "You *are* upset over your low mark, especially when it was unexpected."

One of the most important elements is the questioner's alertness to recognize and to follow leads the student gives. Each interview is a completely new experience, an adventure in human relations. The counselor never knows what is going to develop and must constantly adapt her responses to the individual student. Her real job is so to mobilize her intelligence and social intuition as to be able to make the most helpful response at the right time. This is a skill learned only over a period of time and with much evaluated practice. The counselor can teach herself a good deal by studying her past interviews.

Meeting counselee resistance.—During an interview, the counselor may meet resistance from the student. This may have a number of causes and may take a variety of forms. It may be the result of uncalled-for advice and may take the form of not going to the suggested agency or of making no effort to carry out the suggested plan. It may stem from fear of the counselor's probing, and may be manifested in a refusal to talk or in talk so facetious or irrelevant as to keep the counselor at a distance. Again, as noted above, it may be related to a feeling of guilt at having divulged too much. In some instances, the girl may terminate the interviews, if not overtly, then by the devious methods of forgetting, repeatedly finding it impossible to come, or saying that her problems have all

371.422
Orm

been solved. Persistent tardiness at interviews is sometimes interpreted as resistance; the girl's behavior in other situations would indicate whether that was the case. When she encounters resistance, the counselor should examine her relationship with the girl to see whether she has probed too deeply or tried to rush the girl to a solution. Among the chief unfavorable reactions to interviewing noted in Speer's study (43) were these: "counselor talked too much," "did not treat me as an individual," "tries to force everyone into a mold." Of course, the counselor must refrain from taking the girl's attitude personally; that would cut off all further opportunity for helping her. If the counselor reacts without antagonism and encourages the girl to express her negative feelings, she may remove the resistance.

Closing the interview.—It is usually desirable at the close of an interview or series of interviews to assist the student to sum up the progress she has made and to consider what the next steps should be. The example below shows how one series of interviews ended:

Counselor. Well, do you think we can call it a day? Do you feel ready to go ahead?

Student. Yes, I really think I do. I wouldn't have believed a month ago that things could look so different now. I've tried to figure out how it happened. Somehow, talking the whole thing out got me "unmixed," I guess. I was afraid of my own feelings before, but things are never really so bad when you look at them. Anyway, it had me all tied up in knots so that I couldn't decide anything. Now, I think I know what I ought to do and I'm going ahead and try it, anyway.

Counselor. Fine! I think you also have courage enough to try something else if that doesn't work.

In this case, the girl needed no help in stating her progress.

The recording of interviews.—It is important to keep as accurate a record as possible of all interviews. This will help the counselor to evaluate her own techniques, and also provide a means of studying the student. It is easy to write up routine interviews of which only the salient points need be recorded. But when it is important to preserve the actual words and phrases, there arises the problem of verbatim recording. It sometimes bothers the student to see the counselor writing during an interview, even when the counselor has explained that she needs to have an exact record so that she and the student can study together what they have accomplished. Also, it is very difficult for most counselors to concentrate on the whole situation and write at the same time. Though practice may make this easier, nevertheless, at critical points in the interview when it is of the utmost importance to maintain rapport, the act of writing may interfere. One solution is for the counselor to write a phrase now and then, or a few key words, and then immediately after the interview, make the complete recording. To accomplish this, the counselor must have a schedule which provides adequate time between interviews.

Evaluating the interview.—It is not always easy for the dormitory counselor to determine the success of her interviewing. If some students have made definite educational or vocational plans, she can judge their appropriateness and, to some extent, the effects they have on the girls' adjustment. For example, a student has been able to make what appears to be a reasonable decision regarding her future vocation, and is happy over it. On her own initiative, she has applied for a summer job as trial experience and has been accepted. Further tests of the success of the counseling will come later, but this, at least, is tentative evidence that she has solved her problem with satisfaction to herself. The same thing applies to certain kinds of dormitory difficulties, such as getting on with a roommate. The girl who complained of her roommate's uncooperativeness has achieved some insight into her roommate's behavior and has been able to see that she herself was partly to blame. As a result of her own changed attitude, the other girl's feelings toward her also undergo a change, and both are happy. However, the results of interviews concerned with deeper personality modifications are harder to assess. The girl's own evaluation of the changes in herself is one measure. The judgments of others are also significant, especially those of competent persons who can observe the girl's present functioning, and compare it with her previous behavior in similar situations. These are subjective measures, of course. Moreover, a counselor has no way of being sure that a given change is due to the counseling; some environmental factor may be more important. Despite these hindrances to evaluation, the counselor may always consider these two questions: (1) To what extent has the student's development been furthered? (2) Is she more able to solve her own problems?

SUMMARY

This chapter has described and illustrated the chief techniques used by the dormitory counselor in working with individuals. It has offered suggestions about the uses of tests and the kinds of records which may be kept. There has been a brief discussion of the knowledge and skills used in educational and vocational guidance. Referral procedures have been described. Because of their complexity, the various skills involved in the art of interviewing have received the greatest attention.

Chapter Five

WORKING WITH OTHERS

THIS chapter will consider three ways in which the counselor in the dormitory can increase the effectiveness of her work with the individual: (1) by making use of group activities; (2) by working through individual students; and (3) by seeking the help of other adults, such as deans, doctors, faculty members, or parents, who know or have contact with the girl.

PERSONAL DEVELOPMENT THROUGH GROUP EXPERIENCES IN THE DORMITORY

Nature of Group Work

The complementary relationship between counseling and group work was defined in Chapter One. It was pointed out that in the course of counseling one often finds a girl whose development can be furthered by some group activity or relationship with other girls; likewise, in working with a group, one comes upon individuals with personal problems which might be removed by counseling. In group work with the new emphasis, described by Wilson (58) as an educational process in which the individual is helped to grow emotionally and intellectually by means of a satisfying group experience, and by Strang (47:3) as a "planned, shared experience in which desirable changes take place in member individuals and in the group as a whole," the counselor has an invaluable tool.

Groups on the Campus and in the Dormitory

Groups on the college campus range from the spontaneous, unorganized sort, such as the "bull session" so common in the dormitory, to highly organized groups, often led by adults, such as chapel services and lectures. Groups may demand little or nothing from their members, as do poorly conducted dormitory meetings or some departmental clubs; or they may require a great deal of creative activity, as do certain committees, the glee club or choir, the dramatic and literary societies, the debating union, and the political action groups. As was stated above, the dormitory counselor needs to be familiar with these groups, and should occasionally attend their meetings or performances. Sometimes, through her interest in a certain organization or through participation in sports, she can win over an apparently resistant individual who would not otherwise be accessible to counseling.

In each residence hall there is a governing body, composed typically of elected officers and including, if the hall is large, a council of corridor representatives. Relatively few residents can have the invaluable experience of assuming and carrying through the responsibility of actually running the hall. However, if it is democratically governed, all students have an opportunity, through meetings, to share in making plans. There are usually several committees, and it is through these especially that the counselor can often work to help the girl who needs to find a place for herself. Sometimes scope is provided for wider interests by an activities committee whose function it is to keep attractive bulletin boards, run dormitory art shows or photography exhibits, and get volunteers for community service projects.

Values of Guiding the Student into Beneficial Groups

From a therapeutic standpoint, group activities can give a girl the emotional security of belonging and of wholesome association with the other sex. Girls often develop interests and talents through their participation in a group. Some activities can provide a cause in which a girl may lose herself or experience the satisfaction of performing a useful service. If the group is one in which there is a strong feeling of social consciousness, the student may learn to be less self-centered, may become more interested in the welfare of the group as a whole. By identifying herself with a group whose leaders have prestige, a shy girl may feel that she enhances her own value. Some group associations add greatly to one's zest and interest in life, or give emotional release. Strang (47) pointed out that groups have diagnostic value in that, through participation with others, a girl can see deficiencies in herself—lack of conversational skill or of facility in working with others. Since the counselor must know what a particular girl needs and must be able to help her to make the contact, there is an intimate connection between counseling and placing a girl in a beneficial group.

There are a number of ways in which the dormitory counselor may use activities to help certain girls. She may arrange to have those with special talents asked to take part in dormitory programs. The dormitory office should have a talent file so that program committees may quickly find the names of potential contributors. The experience and recognition which such participation affords, even if it involves only printing signs, may help an isolated girl. Informal discussion groups, on topics suggested by the girls themselves and led by faculty members or the counselor, are helpful. A girl who is too shy to ask a question about a personal problem herself may hear someone else ask such a question, and it is good for her morale to know that others have the same problems. The numerous dormitory social affairs, formal and informal, afford many opportunities for the girl who needs to improve her social skills. In her book on the social program, Stewart (44) has shown in detail how the counselor can help a girl to get this kind of education. Perhaps informal associations are most important of all for personal development: a group gathered around the piano, singing; a few girls preparing refreshments for guests, sunning themselves on the terrace, having an informal discussion in the lounge, or decorating for a dance.

As was mentioned before, the resourceful dormitory coun-

selor can use an endless variety of experiences within the hall
to aid the girls in their self-development. For example, an attractive freshman whose appearance was marred by untidiness
and badly bitten fingernails had applied for waitress work.
In discussing with her the advisability of taking on this extra
responsibility, the counselor mentioned the fact that the careful grooming which it would entail would add some minutes
to the time required for the work. The girl took the hint,
realizing that the job required a neat appearance. Possibly the
resultant improvement in her appearance had some connection
with her increased self-confidence and popularity. To cite
another instance: The dormitory counselor had become rather
well acquainted with an intelligent freshman who had a great
deal of poise and charming manners, but whose attitude toward others in the dormitory, except for two or three close
friends, was rather selfish and intolerant. Her one interest was
music, in which she had some ability. The counselor arranged
to have her put in charge of opera and concert reservations.
Through this activity she became acquainted with others who
were fond of music. She also learned greater patience and
tolerance toward other students. Whereas she herself had
been the sort who hated making plans ahead, she now experienced inconvenience when others gave up reservations at
the last minute. She was intelligent enough to apply these
observations to herself. Such opportunities for counseling
through specific situations are limitless if the counselor is alert
and conscious of the special needs of individual girls.

Need for Flexible Eligibility System

While it is necessary to impose some limitation on the
number of activities in which an individual may engage, and
while those whose academic work is poor cannot afford the
time necessary to hold important offices, the matter of eligi-
bility is often not managed in a wisely flexible manner. Like
other machinery, it may become an end in itself. For example,
a student who is doing poor academic work may especially

need the outlet of singing in the glee club or of taking a minor part in a play, provided she and her counselor can work out a satisfactory schedule insuring adequate time for study. If permitted no outside activity, a student may fritter away some of the extra time at her disposal in such a way as to increase her feeling of futility.

Influence of Group Make-up on Individual Behavior

There is no magic in association with a group per se. Some kinds of group experiences may decrease the confidence of a very insecure girl. Since individuals respond differently to different situations, the group must be the right one for the individual. The writer recalls an intellectually mature girl who had not had the opportunity at her girls' boarding school to meet many boys. She feared ordinary social activities because she lacked small talk. The counselor met her particular need by inviting a few young men with intellectual interests similar to hers to informal fireside discussion groups.

The composition of the group will influence the behavior of the individual in it. Moreno, Jennings, and others have studied these interrelationships. Even though the dormitory counselor's chief concern is not with groups, she would do well to familiarize herself with this material and to try to see its applications to dormitory life. For example, Moreno's studies (31) indicated that, although some students show stable tendencies toward leadership, those who are leaders in one kind of group do not necessarily occupy the same position in another. Similarly isolates in one group may be able in a different group to relate themselves to others. Redl (36), Professor of Social Work at Wayne University, pointed out in a speech that even in a group of ordinary individuals there is such a variety of unknown factors that we cannot tell what group climate will prevail when we put them together; we do not know whether certain attitudes on the part of certain members of the group will be infectious or not. Furthermore, the basic group atmosphere which evolves will determine, in part, whether an individual will behave in a characteristic manner or not. He speaks of the roles that certain individuals play in a group, and of how the distribution of these roles may affect the group adversely or constructively; that is, a group may be swayed by its "professional gripers," or their influence may be offset by that of the "pepper-uppers."

The dormitory counselor may not be able to effect much growth in those highly cohesive voluntary groups known as cliques, which are inevitable in any large dormitory. How-ever, she needs to know their composition, their values, and the effects of their individual members on each other.

She may experiment with the formation of groups by invit-ing selected girls to tea or to the head table in the dining room. In order to create a group which "clicks" and which is appro-priate for the particular student she is trying to help, she needs to know something about the prospective members and their effect on each other; she will avoid inviting a dominating girl who is also a "griper" and who might have a negative effect on the others. Sometimes the counselor will be able to bring together girls known to have strong common interests who will be able to help a timid girl forget her self-conscious-ness and really enjoy the association.

In helping girls to choose their rooms, the counselor may make use of information about group interrelationships. A study by White (57) indicated that locating an unpopular girl in proximity to a popular girl seems to have no effect, in itself, in increasing her popularity. Nevertheless, by using her knowledge of the girls to suggest locations that she feels would result in congenial relationships, the counselor may sometimes aid an individual girl's personality development. For example, a foreign student told the writer she had had trouble getting acquainted with the girls at her preparatory school. When she came to college she had been placed on a corridor with older students. Consequently, she had not made any friends among her own classmates and was beginning to feel left out. When room changes were made, the head of residence saw to it that she was put with some of her own class, especially two girls who were interested in the opportunity to make friends with a girl of a different background. The result was a definite change in her outlook. She was eventually chosen as corridor representative and became one of the best-liked girls in her class. In another case, a shy girl from a small town who had never before been away from home was put near a clique of popular girls. These girls took no interest in her, and she lacked the initiative to make contacts elsewhere. Thus she was acutely unhappy. When the head of residence had her changed to another corridor next to two girls who tried to see that she was included in social activities, she began to look and act like a different person.

The Personnel Point of View for Student Leaders

Many college groups are led by students who need help in acquiring the personnel point of view toward other students. They can gain some notion of the educational possibilities of group experience, though they lack the trained group leader's psychological insight. Many student leaders are so concerned to have their group make a favorable showing that they neglect the personal development of its members. A few, however, can be led to take an interest in the needs of certain girls for social participation and for recognition. The dormitory counselor can work with student leaders in the dormitory to see to it that the social program of the halls helps those who need it most. In their survey of a typical state university campus, Loomis and Green (26) spoke of the great need for activities for the social rejects, who are often not wanted in the existing college organizations.

For example, the social committee of a large residence unit is planning a dance to which a certain number of men from a neighboring university are to be invited. The girls want the dance to be a success, so that their residence hall will get a good reputation with the men's college and the men will wish to come again. Hence, they naturally wish to include only the popular and attractive girls and exclude the "drips," even though the latter have a greater need for the experience. In an actual situation of this kind the committee was brought to see that, since the social program is supposed to serve all the students, they needed to plan other kinds of parties. The girls wisely decided that informal affairs were better, at the beginning, for those who needed social experience. Meanwhile, they enlisted the help of some of the more mature upperclassmen, those interested in going into personnel work, to assist the shy freshmen in taking hold; they showed them how to improve their personal appearance, dress, and conversational ability, or gave them pointers on etiquette. Double dating gave some of them a feeling of security. A physical education instructor gave them dancing lessons. Some of these girls made a definite improvement in social adjustment and personal development. Sometimes even a slight improvement in social adjustment can give a girl the confidence she needs to be a more outgoing person. There may be a small number of deviates who will not respond to this kind of treatment or who will avoid it. Whether such a lack of desire for normal social activity is a form of escape or of defense is not always easy to say. However that may be, some of these students are able to make a happy adjustment through absorption in other kinds of activities, though this adjustment is more easily made in a large and heterogeneous residence unit than in a small house. In any case, student leaders in the dormitory need to be educated to help others achieve a feeling of belonging in some sort of association or activity.

It is not only the socially insecure who need to take part in group activities. All need it for their normal development. Some need it because of inability to work with others, because of emotional tension which requires an outlet, or because of self-centeredness. For example, a freshman, an only child whose every whim has been gratified by overindulgent parents, finds herself disliked by the girls on her corridor because she is inconsiderate and demanding. At the request of the counselor she is asked to serve on a committee, the chairman of which enjoys some prestige and has skill in getting people to work together. The business of the committee is to plan means of enlisting the interest and help of resident girls in the numerous community enterprises that depend on college volunteers. Because of her admiration for the chairman, this freshman works hard and experiences for the first time in her life the satisfactions of rendering a real social service and of working with others. In this case, the counselor's job was to brief the chairman about the girl's need and to give her a suggestion or two about how to give her responsibility. A different situation arises when a young girl is very much in love with a young man of whom her family heartily disapprove, and who she herself knows is not good for her. She finally has the courage to break off the relationship. She finds emotional release in joining a dance group whose student leader is noted for her ability to achieve a remarkable *esprit de corps* and for her friendly interest in each member. In this case, as in the other, the counselor was able to sharpen the student leader's awareness of the possibilities of group therapy. The fact that both these leaders already had interest and skill in human relations made her task easier.

One dormitory leader is convinced in the beginning that a girl named Claire, a sophomore, is a hopeless case. Her sole interest seems to be in playing bridge hour after hour with the same three girls. The counselor is able to show the leader that Claire's development at college need not be despaired of. She has found that Clair has ability in making up skits and putting on entertainments, but that she fears to take the initiative in a large group. The student leader agrees to make her a member of the entertainment committee which attempts to improve the morale of the freshmen during the winter months by putting on skits and organizing parties of various sorts. She is eventually made the chairman of this committee. Her contacts widen and she becomes interested in other aspects of college life. In this instance, the dormitory counselor feels that the student leader is learning as much as the girl.

PERSONAL DEVELOPMENT THROUGH WORKING WITH OTHERS IN THE DORMITORY

In numerous instances, the dormitory counselor needs to work through students as individuals, as well as through those in charge of activities. This has to be done with the greatest care, of course, for students are by no means dependably discreet about keeping confidences. However, the counselor can often secure valuable information from roommates and enlist their cooperation in helping in all sorts of ways. The student adviser, the corridor representative, and mature and sympathetic older students are often resources. Students are pleased to have the counselor place confidence in them by calling them into conference on such matters. By working through these girls, the counselor may not only help the social misfit but also remind those students who have responsibilities to be alert in noticing girls who are not adjusting. Sometimes instead of inquiring about a specific person, the dormitory counselor may ask the adviser about the new students in general. In this way, she may learn about students in need of counseling who have not yet come to her attention. For example, the senior adviser of a transfer student was able to throw further light on the reasons for the girl's inability to make friends, and to give details about her possibly harmful relationship with a boy. The adviser got the girl to discuss her unhappy home situation with the counselor. Eventually, she reached a better adjustment, especially after she had been placed with an understanding roommate. In another instance, the counselor talked with a mature corridor representative about a girl who appeared always to be alone. The representative had noticed the girl's isolation and realized that she should try to do something about it. She promised to invite her to join in activities with the other girls and to try to draw her out. When the counselor remarked that the girl was much interested in dramatics, the corridor representative arranged to have her invited to join the dramatic organization. This she had been too shy to do anything about on her own initiative. As an example of another kind of contact, the counselor might introduce a student to another girl who she feels will be not only congenial, but a helpful influence. The counselor should do this in a casual, seemingly unplanned manner, but in such a way as to enhance the counselee's abilities in the eyes of the other girl. For example: "Oh, Jane, here's a girl I think you'd like to meet. She's spent a summer in Mexico and could help you a lot in your plans for going next summer. And I think you could interest her in helping with that photography exhibit; she seems to be something of an expert."

A head of residence gives the following illustration of how counseling and working through others can reinforce each other:

Martha's difficulty is one that is common among students. She came to my dormitory as a sophomore who had entered college on a brilliant academic record. During her freshman year she had made no friends and had received poor marks. She was so unhappy that she wanted to leave college. With the aid of the Dean she was put where we thought she might make friends. It was a long, slow process for two years. I tried in subtle ways to work her into house groups and encouraged outside dates. She was always glad to talk over with me her sad, lonely state and I discovered a disturbing home situation which I believe was helped by our conversations. Little progress was made, however, until I turned to two key students whom I could trust to be confidential and tactful. With their help, Martha discovered her potentialities. By her senior year she had found a place for herself in the dormitory group and in extracurricular activities as well as a social life outside the college. Her academic work improved and at graduation she had a choice of several good positions.

Student Counselors

The student adviser or counselor is usually an especially good source of help. In almost all colleges, mature and capable students are appointed to assume some responsibility for the counseling of freshmen and advanced-standing students, especially during orientation week. (They are not to be confused with student assistants, usually graduate students, who share in the administrative duties of the halls as members of the staff.) They may be chosen from a list submitted by faculty, personnel officers, and students, sometimes by a small committee composed of students, officers, and deans. Some colleges use seniors; others use juniors and seniors; still others use members of all three upper classes. In some colleges, especially those with large residence units, these counselors are chosen by the residence halls staff and students, and are expected to reside in the halls that choose them. Qualifications vary, but residence heads with whom the writer has talked stress maturity of judgment, good social adjustment, interest in helping students, and loyalty to the values and standards of the college. They are usually chosen in the spring; when they have indicated acceptance of the responsibility, they receive a course of training. This training may be in charge of one of the dormitory counselors or the dean of women. The prospective counselor should get suggestions from former counselors and from the freshmen who have been exposed to the orientation program. Sometimes she will be asked to do some reading on personnel methods. She will attend discussions on the kinds of problems she will be likely to meet. At the Southern Illinois Normal University (56), where juniors are given a two-point-credit course in student personnel administration, students are thereby encouraged to assume these extra duties. However the training is conducted, the student counselors should become aware of their responsibilities.

The functions of the student counselors vary. They are assigned a maximum of fifteen freshmen or advanced-standing students (33) and given a little information about each. They write personal letters of welcome during the summer, and frequently answer questions about various aspects of college life in subsequent letters. They are expected to return to college several days before the arrival of the freshmen to help organize their part of the orientation program. Then they meet the new students—in some colleges at the station; in others, at the dormitory entrance—and in general help them to get acquainted with their physical, human, and academic surroundings. They organize meetings and parties in the dormitory and expeditions about the campus. They strive to inculcate the basic values of college life. They try to deal with any personal problems which arise, such as homesickness, shyness, and general confusion, often talking these over with one of the dormitory counselors. Most of all, they try to give these new students the sense of being a part of a congenial social group as well as of a great institution. In some colleges they are expected to function throughout the year; whether asked to or not, they often do so out of interest. The pamphlet *Residence Halls for Women Students* (33) stated that when they live and work with the freshmen throughout the year, they sometimes receive room rent as compensation. Usually they are asked to submit written reports on the general adjustment and personal characteristics of their advisees.

These student counselors perform an invaluable service for the head of residence, not only by helping new students, but by supplying information about them and by giving a boost to the morale and spirit of the hall through their own enthusiastic interest. Thus they deserve official recognition. They also need to have the feeling that they share equal responsibility for the orientation program with the head of residence and dormitory counselors. They need supervision, of course, but it must not be too obvious.

PERSONAL DEVELOPMENT THROUGH OTHER SERVICES

It has been suggested that the counselor works with the administrative officers and other official personnel. Sometimes the dormitory counselor is a source of information or advice for them; sometimes it is she who seeks them out. On questionnaires sent to twenty-five different colleges, the dean of women or director of residence halls was mentioned most often as a source of help for the counselor. Next in order of frequency was the college doctor; then came the vocational director, psychologist, psychiatrist, testing bureau, and others, in equal ratio. Where the counselor's contacts with faculty are numerous, and unfortunately they are not in some colleges, especially where the faculty commute, she soon finds out which of them can be most useful to her. She can foster this kind of relationship by inviting the most interested members to tea or dinner with small groups of students. Some students have claimed that associations of this kind have meant more to them than anything else in college. Contact between the counselor and a girl's instructor not only gives the counselor valuable information, but often makes the faculty member more interested in the student and more willing to help her.

An example of such a contact follows:

COUNSELOR. It is so good of you to stop in. I hope it wasn't inconvenient.

FACULTY MEMBER. No, indeed. It was just on my way.

COUNSELOR. As I wrote you, I wanted so much to talk to you about Bernice who seems to be doing poorly in your course as well as in her work in general. Do you have any idea what the trouble is? I have some information, but would like more.

FACULTY MEMBER. Well, I have wondered whether she really had the ability to do college work. She seems to be conscientious, but her exams are so poorly written. What have you found?

COUNSELOR. Our records show, on the contrary, that her ability is above the average of students here at college. I tested her myself because in view of her grades I questioned her test record from school. But I noticed that in parts of the test where there was a time limit she got very tense. When I talked to her about her work, she told me that she just went all to pieces on exams. I tried to find out whether it was because she stayed up most of the night before trying to cram the contents of several books into her head, but apparently she does not, and you suggest that her daily preparation is not neglected. I've tried to find out what is at the bottom of this literal *panic* on exams, and as far as I can make out it seems to be connected with her first long exam in high school on which she felt she *had* to do well because her father had said she just must if she ever expected to get to college. He put a lot of pressure on her, and when she did poorly, made her feel that she had disgraced him. She thought she had got over the difficulty, but then it all came back at the beginning of college.

FACULTY MEMBER. The poor child! Why will parents do that sort of thing?

COUNSELOR. Well, it seems he didn't go to college himself and her older sister got married instead of going. So he is determined she shall.

FACULTY MEMBER. But fortunately, she has the ability if only we can help it to function. What do you think I can do?

COUNSELOR. Have you talked with Bernice at all?

FACULTY MEMBER. No, only casually. I have intended to ask her to come for an interview, but waited, hoping she'd come in answer to the general invitation I gave.

COUNSELOR. I don't know why she hasn't, for she has said she thinks you're a fine teacher. But I imagine it's because she is ashamed of her exam papers. She thinks she's a complete failure. Perhaps you could call her in and encourage her to talk about how she feels when she takes an exam and also make her feel that she isn't completely hopeless. I am sure that you could do that better than I. If you could build up her confidence so that she could do well on just one exam, I believe the battle would be almost won.

FACULTY MEMBER. I wish I'd known about this before. Anyway, I'm glad you told me now and I'll certainly see her. Then I'll let you know how it works out, and meanwhile if you learn anything else, let me know.

COUNSELOR. Indeed I shall. I do so appreciate your cooperation. I only wish I had been on my toes earlier about this, but Bernice is the quiet type who easily escapes notice and she just happened to be one of the few with whom I did not have interviews at the beginning of the year. Her school record, unfortunately, gave no hint of this; otherwise, we might have prevented it.

A few days later the girl came to the counselor, with whom by now she felt a friendly relationship. She said she had just had a nice talk with the teacher and felt much better about her work. She really thought that she was going to be able to overcome her difficulty. The next examination proved that she could. It should be noted here that there might have been a deeper problem in her relationship with her father, but subsequent adjustment on the girl's part did not seem to indicate that there was.

Case Conferences

If a student is having a hard time adjusting, and especially if there seems to be some question of the desirability of her remaining in college, one of the administrative officers will probably call a meeting at which all who have pertinent information about the girl can pool it and try to decide how to help her. The dormitory counselor has much to contribute to the case conference. Strang (46) has pointed out that one of the values of this procedure lies in the in-service education in personnel work which it provides for the faculty and other members of the staff who attend. It is unfortunate that some administrators call case conferences only when it is time to dismiss a girl, rather than early enough so that means might be found of avoiding such a step.

The Dormitory Counselor's Relationship with Parents

For obvious reasons, the counselor in a residence hall does not have numerous contacts with parents. When she does have a conference with a student's parents, she should in most cases secure the student's approval and sometimes should arrange to have her participate. If the counselor is to see the parents alone for the purpose of trying to interpret the girl's viewpoint or to get their approval for some plan, she may talk over with the girl the important points to be covered. If the counselor talks to the parents without the girl's knowledge, the latter is likely to feel that the counselor is an ally of the parents against her, a feeling that is naturally not conducive to a good counseling relationship. In talking with the parents, the counselor must be careful not to be prejudiced by her sympathy with the girl's viewpoint. A counselor is perhaps prone to blame all of a student's difficulties on her parents, and to forget that they are people with problems, too, and that they know the girl better than she does. Of course, parents find it difficult to be objective about their children. It is often harder to accept limitations in a daughter than in oneself. In cases where the mother has not really wanted the child, her subsequent sense of guilt may have caused her to lean over backwards to protect her or do too much for her. The suggestion that she may actually be hindering the girl by her efforts amounts almost to a threat to her peace of conscience. It is also hard for a mother to allow her daughter to grow up, to grow away from her. The counselor may be able to help her see that this is a necessary part of her daughter's attaining independence. At the same time the counselor can reassure her that, though her daughter may give the appearance of not needing her, she still does need her understanding and affection. Sometimes a counselor can help a girl more, indirectly, by understanding a parent's feelings, than by actually discussing the girl's problem with the parents.

Fathers should realize that they, too, have an important role in relation to their daughters. Bingham (3) said that girls need their fathers' open approval and admiration of them as women to help them accept the feminine role. If fathers ignore this fact and demand high academic success as the sole price of their approval, they may unwittingly be making their daughters' future adjustment to marriage more difficult.

There are a few parents who try to "use" the counselor to punish the girl, to check up on her, or to put pressure on her. They may ask the counselor to write once a week to report on the girl's progress. This the counselor must refuse to do, explaining tactfully and patiently her function in relation to the girl. The writer had some experience with a parent who had evidently been in the habit of staging a scene whenever her daughter got into academic difficulties at preparatory school;

she flew on from the west to hire tutors and see to it that the
administration checked on her daughter constantly, and afterwards continued the attack by frequent phone calls and wires.
The daughter rather enjoyed this attention and saw to it that
she got it by coasting along until a crisis arose. She was a very
intelligent girl who had been sent off to boarding school when
rather young; hence she felt that she had been cheated out of
normal contact with her family. In this case, the mother got
some insight into her daughter's need for attention, and the
daughter, too, achieved some self-understanding.

The following interview with a parent illustrates one way
of meeting a common problem:

COUNSELOR. Good afternoon, Mrs. Matthews. I am so glad you
could come. I have been interested in trying to help Jean and I
felt that you, who know her so much better than I, could give
me some cues. She's a fine girl with really good potentialities, but,
as you know, her work continues to be poor and I don't feel that
she is happy in the dormitory. So far, my efforts to help don't
seem to have got anywhere.

MRS. MATTHEWS. I'm glad to hear you say that she has potentialities. I was beginning to feel that she was a hopeless case. It
seems to me that I have done everything to stimulate that girl,
but she never shows interest in anything. My husband and I are
great readers and she's grown up in an atmosphere of books and
music. But I have to drive her to read a book and she'll never go
with us to concerts. She's so different from her younger sister
who'll be coming here in two years, by the way. You won't have
any trouble with her. But Jean—honestly, I don't know what is
wrong with her-

COUNSELOR. Can it be that she lacks confidence and covers it
up with this air of boredom and indifference? I have felt that she
doesn't want to try to do things because she's afraid she'll fail if
she does.

MRS. MATTHEWS. I don't know why she should. We've always
told her she could do things if she tried.

COUNSELOR. I'm sure you've done a great deal to try to encourage her and it must be very discouraging to you to see so little
result from your efforts.

MRS. MATTHEWS. Indeed it is. My husband and I feel that we
have failed [with a sigh]. But maybe we have handled her in the

wrong way. We may have pushed her too much. She was our first and we probably felt she *had* to do us credit. Perhaps we've tried to stuff culture down her throat.

COUNSELOR. That could be, with the best of intentions. Many teachers, as well as parents, don't realize that girls need a chance to be themselves. But tell me, do she and this bright young sister get on well together?

MRS. MATTHEWS. We've never allowed them to fight. They appear to get on well, but I can't say they seem too fond of each other. It's possible Jean's nose got a little out of joint because her sister was such a sweet child and maybe I, without knowing it, made too big a fuss over her. But really, the younger one isn't the favorite. Except that others, outside, always made much of her: her grandmother, for one, and the teachers. Actually, I've given Jean more attention in the last ten years because she always needed prodding. But sometimes—I hate to admit it—I've thought she almost hated me.

COUNSELOR. It's not unusual, Mrs. Matthews, for daughters to appear to dislike their parents at times. She loves you, too, you may be sure of that, though she may have queer ways of showing it. But you show unusual understanding of the way her younger sister's popularity might make Jean feel. Sometimes it is so hard not to indicate, without saying a word, that you are so pleased with one child and not with another. Maybe she resented her sister's imagined superior status all the more because she couldn't fight with her.

MRS. MATTHEWS. That's possible. And another thing's occurred to me. Maybe she's tried to get attention from me by not being as I wanted her.

COUNSELOR. I wouldn't be surprised if you were right.

They went on to discuss how they might help the girl. The point to note is that, though the counselor probably saw at once the mistakes the parents had made, she avoided antagonizing the mother by pointing them out; she waited for the mother to see them herself. She also reflected the mother's feeling of discouragement. This counselor was fortunate to be dealing with a parent who was so intelligent and well balanced that she gained insight quickly.

Much of the counselor's contact with parents will be by letter. Here again, it is well if the girl knows approximately what the counselor writes, except in rare instances where it would harm her to know. Sometimes the counselor will write merely to assure a distant parent that her daughter is making a satisfactory adjustment, all things considered. This may be especially helpful if a girl is making lower grades than she did in high school because of differences in standards and methods of instruction. Sometimes the counselor may write to give the facts about some difficulty a daughter has been involved in and to explain what the girl is now planning to do. It is risky to write detailed explanations of the reasons behind a girl's behavior, especially in psychological terms, since what one writes is so likely to be misunderstood. It surely does no harm to stress a girl's strong points, especially if one has a notion that she is not appreciated. It is unnecessary to say that, whatever one writes, the utmost clarity, tactfulness, and honesty are essential—and that carbon copies of the letters must be kept.

CONCLUSION

In this chapter an attempt has been made to describe and illustrate the various avenues through which the dormitory counselor may work to reinforce or supplement her counseling contacts with individual students: the use of group activities, of the experiences for growth in the dormitory, of contacts with student leaders, and of associations with other interested adults on the campus. All are significant as they enter into the student's development.

Chapter Six

A DORMITORY COUNSELOR'S
QUALIFICATIONS AND RESPONSIBILITIES

As was pointed out in Chapter One, the new concept of residence halls as agencies of social education and counseling centers necessarily affects the traditional concepts of the qualifications and functions of persons in charge of residence halls. "Good disciplinarian" and "nice woman who loves young people" are no longer adequate standards. In this chapter an attempt will be made to describe the responsibilities of a head of residence in her role of counselor, and the personal and professional qualifications which she needs. The sort of person the dormitory counselor is, and the skills and knowledge her training and experience have given her, are obviously of paramount importance.

DESIRABLE TRAITS IN A HEAD OF RESIDENCE

Thompson (53) said that to outline the traits that make an effective head resident would be as difficult as to describe the traits of a successful teacher. Despite the obstacles to this sort of analysis, *Residence Halls for Women Students* (33) stressed such personal qualities as good moral character, personal dignity, and emotional stability. Next in importance are a sincere interest in young people, the ability to hold their respect and good will, and active cultural interests which can enrich the lives of the dormitory students.

The writer feels that mature and impartial judgment is a very necessary characteristic, since the counselor must sometimes act in matters that have great importance for individual girls. The need for sympathetic objectivity has been pointed out in a previous chapter. Warmth of manner and sensitivity to people's feelings are important in producing the sort of atmosphere wherein students will feel free to talk. The counselor should be a friendly, gracious person, at home in any social situation. She should like people in large as well as in small groups, in formal settings as well as in informal. She should be able to influence public opinion, not by exhortation, but by her subtle guidance of student leaders. She should be able to work harmoniously with other adults as well as with students. Her own personal adjustment should be reasonably satisfactory. She would not be human if she did not have problems, but she must be aware of her own motivations and must not use counseling to satisfy her own need for intimate relationships or for domination. She should have the ability to laugh at herself, and should not let herself get too wrought up over the girls' problems. As Lloyd-Jones (25) said, it is better to be a little too optimistic than to be overanxious and overeager; after all, college students are a selected group with better than average capacity for self-direction. The counselor must have faith in this capacity, as has been said before. She must respect students as near-adults, and take a genuine interest and pleasure in the way their minds work. She needs to be flexible and open-minded about their viewpoints, but, at the same time, to have well-established values and standards. Just as girls need to know where their parents stand on certain moral issues, so they need to feel this stability in those who sometimes act in place of parents. The counselor should be deeply concerned about religious and spiritual values, able to apply a religious philosophy to the vexed problems of human relations and the challenging questions raised by young people. Confidence in her own ability to help is important; if she is afraid the student will not respond or will feel that she is inquisitive, the girl is likely to sense this fact and be affected

In addition to the cultural interests mentioned above, the

dormitory counselor should be well read and well informed
on current affairs, and should have a strong sense of civic responsibility. In discussions on an intellectual plane, she should
be able to hold her own with the various members of the college faculty.

A personal qualification that needs discussion is that of age.
When the residence unit is small and the head of residence is
on her own most of the time, an older person can more easily
meet the emergencies calling for mature judgment and experience. *Residence Halls for Women Students* (33) made the
point that freshmen find the transition easier if a woman about
the same age as their mothers presides over the house. There
is an advantage in having a woman who has been happily married and who has had children. An older woman usually finds
it easier to command the respect of parents and administrative
officers. She can accommodate herself more easily to the
schedule of working hours; a young person finds it harder to
give up evenings and week ends. However, in a large residence unit where there are several counselors, it is desirable
to have some young people among them; the young have an
enthusiasm that can capture the loyalty of students. Proximity in age also gives them a better understanding of certain
student problems. A young counselor must be careful, however, not to become completely "one of the girls"; she must
maintain a certain reticence. From the standpoint of intrastaff
companionships, it is desirable to have more than one counselor in each age group. From the standpoint of the students,
too, it is an advantage to have both younger and older counselors; some students find it easier to approach young counselors and others, older ones.

Freshman Study of Traits Most Appreciated

In order to find out what students felt were the most desirable qualities in the sort of counselor to whom they would
respond, the freshmen in a large residence unit of a liberal arts
college were asked soon after their arrival in the fall to weigh

certain items in order of their importance. The item checked most frequently was "has natural, friendly manner; makes you feel at ease"; next came "is sincere and frank—does not try to 'put anything over' "; then, "is always consistent and fair in treatment of the girls"; and fourth, "is always open-minded and considerate of student opinion." The item of the questionnaire checked least often was "makes you feel important; stresses your strong points." Perhaps the wording of this item was unfortunate; the freshmen felt that they should not admit a desire to feel important. "Is a stimulating conversationalist with a variety of interests" and "well groomed, attractive" also received few votes. When asked to add other qualities which they thought important, the freshmen gave these responses: "treats us like adults," "has objective viewpoint," "has much patience," "does not make you feel sorry you have confided," "intelligence and ingenuity," and "reliability." The transfer students and seniors and sophomores, the same group referred to in Chapter Two, while they were not given the same questionnaire, gave the impression from responses to other questions that they thought the counselor should be a friendly, sympathetic, understanding person to whom it was easy to talk, who treated girls as individuals and as adults, and who worked cooperatively with them in making plans for the dormitory. The transfer students, asked to mention any qualities they had disliked in former counselors, mentioned unfairness, favoritism ("seeing too much of certain girls who tended to haunt the office"), unnatural manner, "psychological approach" (undefined), too great aggressiveness in helping, and lack of respect for a girl's reticence. It is interesting that the pattern of traits which emerge from the freshman study, where the students were asked to choose from among twenty items, is very similar to that suggested by the other students in their free responses. This fact would seem to suggest that it is possible to generalize concerning the type of counselor that girls prefer and the training and experience that are needed for the work.

NECESSARY AND DESIRABLE TRAINING
AND EXPERIENCE

A college education is essential for the head of residence in order that she may have an intellectual background similar to that of the girls. In addition, she should have, or be working toward, professional preparation such as that represented by a master's degree in the field of student personnel work. This would include courses in student personnel administration, adolescent psychology, vocational guidance, and group work techniques, including training in the leading of discussions. Some training in the theory and practice of testing and in remedial reading is also desirable. It is highly recommended that the counselor take an in-service training course in which her recorded interviews with students and her work as a whole can be constructively criticized from time to time. Supervised counseling in a guidance clinic dealing with the problems of normal young people would be invaluable in giving her a firsthand understanding of the dynamics of behavior, especially if it could be continued long enough to afford her the feeling of some professional competence.

Residence Halls for Women Students (33) mentioned as a requirement for counselors successful experience in directing groups of young people, through teaching or other leadership positions. The writer feels that some kind of experience in an educational institution which would provide some insight into the teaching-learning process is highly desirable. While, as was pointed out in Chapter Three, the academic mind has a tendency, which needs to be checked, to advise or dictate, some experience in education, on either the secondary or college level, is important. Experience with high school students, not necessarily teaching, makes it easier to understand freshman problems. Working cooperatively with students in extracurricular activities is probably the most relevant experience a counselor can have. Group work, professional or volunteer, such as Girl Scouts, Y.W.C.A., club work in settlements, or other community activities is also very useful background. It is desirable that the counselor have almost any kind of experience which would contribute toward making her a more interesting and vital personality, give her contact with a variety of people, and provide her an opportunity to exercise leadership.

In venturing to set up these personal and professional qualifications as either necessary or desirable, the writer realizes that she is treating a controversial subject where there is considerable difference of opinion and where practice lags far behind theory. However, since the modern educational viewpoint recognizes the "social curriculum" of the dormitory as an intrinsic part of the students' education, equally important as the academic curriculum, it follows that those who carry on the counseling and the group work in the dormitory should be as well trained as other members of the faculty and should enjoy faculty standing. *Residence Halls for Women Students* (33) supported these recommendations in the main, though not in detail.

PLANS FOR DORMITORY ORGANIZATION

Some colleges select members of the faculty who are especially gifted with ability to work with students, release them from a part of their teaching duties, and appoint each as a part-time dormitory counselor or head of a small hall with an assistant. The teaching contact these counselors have with students increases their understanding of academic problems. Because they have faculty status, they are usually a more effective liaison between the faculty or college dean and the students. If they have some personnel training, in addition to their academic training, this arrangement may be very satisfactory. The drawback is that since their interest is divided between counseling and teaching, one of these responsibilities may be neglected at times. Their teaching schedule may make it difficult for them to attend to some of the critical problems which arise in the dormitory at the most unpredictable moments. The plan works best in a small and informal residence unit where everyone knows everyone else.

In some institutions the counselors are graduate students taking in-service training at the same or a neighboring university, and the head of residence is a fully trained, full-time personnel worker. Since dormitory counseling lends itself to working on a part-time basis, this organization has proved to be practical, provided the graduate students are not carrying too heavy an academic load. The disadvantage of giving this work exclusively to graduate students is that there is too frequent a turnover of counselors.

Where there are several counselors in a large residence unit, each may assume special responsibility for a certain group of girls, such as one floor, or one class, at the same time sharing in the responsibility for the general administration of the dormitory and thus having contact with all the girls in the hall. Another plan is to allocate special functions: one counselor will deal with vocational counseling and testing; another, the social program; a third, the student government. This plan utilizes the special training and interests of each counselor.

In some liberal arts colleges with small dormitories one woman is head of the house, often assisted by a resident faculty member. Sometimes these heads are specially trained; sometimes it is the policy of the college to select those who are personally suited to the position, regardless of training. The more homelike character of these residences makes it easier to spot students who need referrals and to arrange them. It is possible, too, that fewer problems arise there than in the large, impersonal units, or that they can be anticipated and prevented more easily. Nevertheless, these girls ask the same kinds of questions and have the same needs for developmental and remedial counseling. While it is sound procedure to choose these heads on the basis of suitable personal qualifications, if they also have some professional training they can be even more helpful to the girls.

In a very few small colleges the dormitories are completely unsupervised except for the presence of a student officer. In these colleges all the counseling, except that referred to the psychiatric staff, is handled by the girls' faculty advisers. Counseling and instruction belong to the educational program.

There are other plans which combine certain features of the four already mentioned. However, these four are representative of a large number of colleges. It is not possible to recommend one in preference to the others. In the first place, there is almost no evidence as to how well they actually function. Even if there were, each residence unit would still have to work out the arrangement which best fitted its particular needs. It can be confidently stated, however, that more and more colleges are recognizing residence hall counseling as a professional job demanding trained personnel and recognition by the faculty.

STUDENT ASSISTANTS

In many colleges and universities young graduate students work part time as administrative assistants. They carry on some of the functions of the residence halls office, such as permissions and night duty, and assist with the social program, thus freeing the trained counselors for actual counseling. They are usually remunerated by scholarships or fellowships. According to a survey made in 1946 by the Residence Halls Staff at Stanford University, they are chosen on the basis of such qualifications as interest in personnel work, ability to work well with students, maturity of judgment, scholarship, and personal appearance and taste. Their work serves as valuable in-service training, especially where it is properly directed by the dean or head of residence. Some of these student assistants later become full-time counselors. They are often extremely helpful in boosting the spirit of the hall and in keeping grievances from developing because they have an intimate understanding of the students' point of view.

THE WORK OF THE COUNSELOR
OR HEAD OF RESIDENCE

Because this book is intended for the use of prospective as well as acting counselors, it may be well to offer an analysis of what the work entails. Some of the following functions have been mentioned before in the descriptions of the skills needed for counseling: (1) becoming acquainted with all members of the house group, (2) being available to students for consultation, (3) helping students in various emergencies, such as illness and personal difficulties, (4) coordinating the information about the student on the personnel record, (5) acting as a consultant for others concerned with the student, (6) helping to train student advisers, (7) working with student government officers and with committees for the maintenance of good government and harmonious living in the hall, (8) helping to direct freshman orientation, (9) assisting in assigning rooms and in adjusting difficulties with room arrangements, (10) referring students to experts, (11) meeting parents, and (12) reporting student and dormitory problems to the office to which the counselor is responsible.

In addition to these functions, most of which are related to counseling, the head of residence will assist in the social program, act as social hostess, help students to acquire social skills, make out the social program, help plan the freshman handbook, if there is one, in cooperation with student officers and the dean, and attend meetings of the residence hall staff to which she is expected to contribute ideas for the better running of the hall as well as information about students.

There are certain business details to which the head of residence must give attention: making the dormitory budget, planning for physical changes in the rooms, making requisitions for general supplies, making up office forms, and working with the housekeeper and students to create surroundings that are as artistic, hygienic, orderly, and homelike as available funds permit. While in most colleges the head of residence will not have meal-planning responsibilities, she will surely need to work with the dietitian, not only because the meals have importance in relation to the health and social life of the girls, but also because the dietitian is often the employer of some of the students. With the college doctor she will share responsibility for the health of the girls.

In a large residence unit there is a certain amount of office work connected with the job: authorizing or checking on permissions, making sure that all girls are accounted for daily, acting as a source of general information about the college to visitors and prospective students, and making certain that the girls are informed about a variety of administrative matters. In some residence halls the counselors probably spend too much time on clerical work which could better be assigned to a good secretary. However, the counselor learns a great deal about the students through these office contacts and so perhaps is better able to keep her finger on the pulse of the dormitory life.

It is obviously impossible to mention all the specific jobs which a head of residence performs, since these vary from college to college and even from week to week. In situations in which two or more personnel workers are employed in a dormitory, the responsibilities of the person designated as dormitory counselor are less extensive than those of the head of residence, with more emphasis on the counseling duties. Since this book is intended for all personnel workers in women's dormitories, this highly simplified description of the work includes the functions which the one solely in charge of the personnel work in the dormitory usually performs.

The resident aspect of this work need not be a disadvantage if the living quarters of the dormitory head are somewhat apart from the students', as they should be, and if she has time to herself and some facilities for entertaining in her own rooms. To be sure, she must be available to the students much of the time. Those who like to have large blocks of free time may not be happy in this work. However, there are many compensations to offset what some may consider the disadvantage of living on the job.

SIGNIFICANCE AND IMPORTANCE OF THE WORK

Possibly there are few positions which call for more varied personal and professional qualifications or which are more demanding of energy, intelligence, resourcefulness, and spiritual stamina. Certainly there are few which can be more challenging or more rewarding. Work with students of college age is always fascinating, and college contacts are intellectually stimulating. The task of helping these young people to develop their potentialities and to become finer individuals, prepared to give their best to life, is an exciting one.

Many colleges still think of their residence halls chiefly as housing units. Crowded postwar conditions on campuses have tended to give undue emphasis to physical aspects. More and more emphasis must be placed on creating a mental climate that facilitates the growth of the individual as a person and as a socially responsible group member. Both the social program and counseling are needed to secure these values.

As Professor Mayo of Harvard University wrote:

We have failed to train students in the study of social situations; we have thought that first-class technical training was sufficient in a modern and mechanical age. As a consequence we are technically competent as no other age in history has been; and we combine this with utter social incompetence. This defect of education and administration has of recent years become a menace to the whole future of civilization (30:13).

Since dormitories are natural centers for education in the art of human relations, and since counseling aims to liberate the individual from her fears, worries, and other limitations, this work of the dormitory counselor assumes great significance. By means of it, students are helped to become happier, more adequate persons and hence cooperative and contributing members of a social group.

Bibliography

*1. BENNETT, M. E. *College and Life. Problems of Self-discovery and Self-direction* (revised edition). New York: McGraw-Hill Book Company, 1947.

*2. BINGHAM, Walter Van Dyke. *Aptitudes and Aptitude Testing*, pp. 245–265. New York: Harper and Brothers, 1937.

*3. ——. *How to Interview* (third edition). New York: Harper and Brothers, 1941.

4. BIRD, Charles, and BIRD, Dorothy M. *Learning More by Effective Study*. New York: D. Appleton-Century Company, 1945.

5. BUROS, Oscar K. *The Third Mental Measurements Yearbook*. New Brunswick, N. J.: Rutgers University Press, 1949.

6. CHASSEL, Joseph. "Individual Counseling of College Students," *Journal of Consulting Psychology*, 4 (November–December, 1940), 205–209.

7. COLE, Luella. *Background for College Teaching*. New York: Farrar and Rinehart, 1940.

8. CURRAN, Charles A. *Personality Factors in Counseling*. New York: Greene and Stratton, 1945.

*9. ELLIOTT, Grace Loucks. *Understanding the Adolescent Girl*. New York: Henry Holt and Company, 1930.

*10. FOSTER, Robert G., and WILSON, Pauline P. *Women After College. A Study of the Effectiveness of Their Education*. New York: Columbia University Press (for the Merrill-Palmer School), 1942.

*11. GARRETT, Annette. *Interviewing: Its Principles and Methods*. New York: Family Welfare Association of America, 1942.

12. GOOD, Carter V. (editor). *A Guide to Colleges, Universities, and Professional Schools*. Washington, D. C.: American Council on Education, 1946.

13. HARTSHORNE, Hugh (editor). *From School to College*. New Haven, Conn. Yale University Press, 1939.

14. HAWKES, H. E., and HAWKES, A. R. *Through a Dean's Open Door*. New York: McGraw-Hill Book Company, 1945.

*15. HAYES, Harriet. *Planning Residence Halls*. New York: Bureau of Publications, Teachers College, Columbia University, 1932.

16. HEATH, Clark W. *What People Are*. Cambridge, Mass.: Harvard University Press, 1945.

* The starred references are those especially valuable for the dormitory counselor.

17. HEATON, Kenneth L., and WEEDON, Vivian. *The Failing Student.* Chicago: The University of Chicago Press, 1939.

*18. HOLLINGWORTH, Leta S. *Psychology of the Adolescent.* New York: D. Appleton-Century Company, 1928.

*19. HORNEY, Karen. *Our Inner Conflicts.* New York: W. W. Norton Company, 1945.

*20. JONES, Arthur J. *Principles of Guidance* (third edition). New York: McGraw-Hill Book Company, 1945.

21. KAMAROVSKY, M. "Cultural Contradictions and Sex Roles," *American Journal of Sociology,* 52 (1946), 184–189.

22. LANDIS, Paul H. *Adolescence and Youth.* New York: McGraw-Hill Book Company, 1945.

23. LIND, Melva. "The College Dormitory as an Emerging Force in New Education," *Association of American Colleges Bulletin,* 32 (December, 1946), 529–538.

24. LINTON, Ralph. *The Cultural Background of Personality.* New York: D. Appleton-Century Company, 1945.

*25. LLOYD-JONES, Esther McD., and SMITH, Margaret Ruth. *A Student Personnel Program for Higher Education.* New York: McGraw-Hill Book Company, 1938.

26. LOOMIS, Stuart D., and GREEN, Arnold W. "The Patterns of Mental Conflict in a Typical State University," *Journal of Abnormal and Social Psychology,* 42 (July, 1947), 342–355.

27. McCALL, William A., BALCH, and HERRING. *You and College.* New York: Harcourt, Brace and Company, 1936.

28. McCLOSKY, Terry, and Scott (editors). *What College Offers.* New York: F. S. Crofts and Company, 1941.

29. McCULLOUGH, Constance, STRANG, Ruth, and TRAXLER, Arthur. *Problems in the Improvement of Reading.* New York: McGraw-Hill Book Company, 1946.

30. MAYO, Elton. *The Social Problems of an Industrial Civilization.* Cambridge, Mass.: Division of Research, Graduate School of Business Administration, Harvard University, 1945.

31. MORENO, J. L. *Who Shall Survive?* Nervous and Mental Diseases Monograph, No. 58. New York: Nervous and Mental Disease Publishing Company, 1934.

*32. MORGAN, John J. B. *Keeping a Sound Mind.* New York: The Macmillan Company, 1939.

*33. National Association of Deans of Women. *Residence Halls for Women Students.* Washington, D. C.: The Association, 1947.

34. NEILSON, William Allan (editor). *Roads to Knowledge* (revised edition). New York: W. W. Norton and Company, 1937.

35. *Occupational Index.* New York: Occupational Index, Inc., New York University, published quarterly.

36. REDL, Fritz. "Discipline and Group Psychology," *Journal of National Association of Deans of Women* 11 (October, 1947), 3–15.

*37. ROGERS, Carl. *Counseling and Psychotherapy*. Boston: Houghton Mifflin Company, 1936.

38. ROSE, A. A. "The Effect of War on the Social and Emotional Adjustment of College Girls," *Journal of Social Psychology*, 24 (August, 1946), 177–185.

39. SCHLEMAN, Helen B. "Women's Housing," *Journal of the National Association of Deans of Women*, 11, No. 1 (October, 1947), 31–39.

*40. SEARS, Laurence. *Responsibility*. New York: Columbia University Press, 1932.

*41. SHAFFER, L. F. *The Psychology of Adjustment*. Boston: Houghton Mifflin Company, 1936.

42. SNYDER, William A. "An Investigation of the Nature of Nondirective Therapy," *Journal of General Psychology*, 33 (1945), 193–224.

43. SPEER, G. E. "Negative Reactions to College Counseling," *Occupations*, 13 (November 7, 1945).

*44. STEWART, Helen Q. *Some Social Aspects of Residence Halls for Women*. New York: Professional and Technical Press, 1942.

*45. STRANG, Ruth. *Counseling Technics in College and Secondary School* (revised and enlarged). New York: Harper and Brothers, 1949.

*46. ——. *Educational Guidance: Its Principles and Practice*. New York: The Macmillan Company, 1947.

*47. ——. *Group Activities in Colleges and Secondary Schools* (revised). New York: Harper and Brothers, 1946.

48. ——. *Study Type of Reading Exercises*. New York: Bureau of Publications, Teachers College, Columbia University, 1935.

49. SUPER, Donald E. *Appraising Vocational Fitness by Means of Psychological Tests* (first edition). New York: Harper and Brothers, 1949.

50. TAFT, Jessie. *The Dynamics of Therapy in a Controlled Relationship*. New York: The Macmillan Company, 1933.

*51. TAYLOR, Katherine. *Do Adolescents Need Parents?* New York: D. Appleton-Century Company, 1938.

*52. THOM, Douglas A. *Normal Youth and Its Everyday Problems*. New York: D. Appleton-Century Company, 1932.

53. THOMPSON, Florence M. "The Use of Dormitories for Social Education," *Educational and Psychological Measurement*, 7 (Autumn 1947, Part II), 648–654.

54. TRIGGS, Frances O. *Improve Your Reading*. Minneapolis: University of Minnesota Press, 1942.

55. WECHSLER, David. *The Measurement of Adult Intelligence*. Baltimore: The Williams and Wilkins Company, 1944.

56. WHARTON, Mildred M. (compiler). *Orientation of Freshmen in Colleges and Universities*. Washington, D. C.: National Association of Deans of Women, 1942.

57. WHITE, Helen Walker. "Counseling Women Students," *Journal of Higher Education*, 18, No. 6 (June, 1947), 312.

*58. WILSON, Gertrude. *Group Work and Case Work: Their Relationship* *and Practice*. New York: Family Welfare Association of America, 1941.

59. WRENN, C. Gilbert, and LARSEN, Robert P. *Studying Effectively*. Stanford University, Calif.: Stanford University Press, 1941.

*60. ZACHRY, Caroline B. *Emotion and Conduct in Adolescence*. New York: D. Appleton-Century Company, 1940.

Appendix A

QUESTIONNAIRE FOR DORMITORY STUDENTS

Part I. *a.* How can a residence hall director or her assistants best serve the students? *b.* What should she *not* do? (Write below. Use the back if you need more space.)

Part II. Please rate these items on a scale as follows: (Put the number in the parentheses to the left of the margin.)

4—"should by all means see that this is done; is of primary importance"
3—"important; should be done if possible"
2—"desirable, but of less importance"
1—"not important; immaterial whether done or not"
0—"should not be attempted"

If you think an item unimportant or undesirable, I should appreciate your saying why. You may write qualifications or comments on others.

The person in charge of a residence hall (or her assistants) should:
( ) 1. be available to talk with the girls regarding any personal matters.
( ) 2. collect detailed information on the background of each girl.
( ) 3. have her own living room, as well as her office, open for the girls to drop in informally.
( ) 4. help each student to appraise her own assets and liabilities.
( ) 5. give an opportunity for girls with special talents to use them in dormitory activities.
( ) 6. help girls to feel "accepted" and to achieve some feeling of "belonging."
( ) 7. encourage every student to participate in some college activity.

( ) 8. provide "marriage counseling" (trained outsider) for engaged girls.

( ) 9. help student to achieve independence of her family.

( ) 10. help student to form better health habits.

( ) 11. give girls help in religious orientation and development of philosophy of life.

( ) 12. help girls gain insight into their own personalities by giving one or more personality tests.

( ) 13. tell girl the proper solution when she asks for help on a difficulty that she has encountered.

( ) 14. encourage girls to speak very frankly by not passing judgment on their conduct.

( ) 15. give instruction to girls who need it as to how to make the most of their personal appearance, posture, hair, etc.

( ) 16. when talking to students on personal matters, allow them to do most of the talking and to take the initiative in working out a solution to their difficulties.

( ) 17. see that girls who have no men friends have opportunity for meeting suitable men.

( ) 18. make a point of getting to know the men friends of the girls.

( ) 19. help girls who do not make friends easily to improve their techniques of making social contacts.

( ) 20. establish a strong personal relationship with the girls by doing such things as visiting the girls in their rooms, celebrating birthdays, etc.

( ) 21. try to break up cliques among girls by encouraging regrouping.

( ) 22. give girls who need to develop responsibility a chance to assume some.

( ) 23. try to make the social program contribute to the personal development of each girl.

( ) 24. give vocational and aptitude tests.

( ) 25. help students to explore various vocations with the view of finding the one which best suits her interests and abilities.

( ) 26. invite experts in the various vocational fields for the girls to consult.

( ) 27. help the girls to find and follow up opportunities for summer jobs.

( ) 28. help the girls who need it to analyze their study habits and make a plan for more effective procedures in the future.

( ) 29. help the girls who need it to plan their time better by the use of a daily schedule.

( ) 30. give diagnostic reading test and remedial help if desired.

( ) 31. talk with student's instructors to find out how she can best help with academic difficulties.

( ) 32. invite the faculty for meals and to meet the girls in small groups afterwards.

( ) 33. help to develop leadership by assisting the student government and various committees in the dorm to function effectively.

( ) 34. invite the parents for certain special functions in the dormitory.

( ) 35. confer with parents to find out more about a student's background and (sometimes) to help parents understand girls better.

( ) 36. attend as many as possible of the meetings and other affairs in which dormitory girls participate.

( ) 37. encourage group solidarity within classes: all-freshmen parties, etc.

( ) 38. stimulate girls not working to capacity to put forth greater effort.

( ) 39. encourage the following of the old traditions of the college and the creating of new ones.

( ) 40. decide each disciplinary case with reference to the needs and background of the one who has committed the misdemeanor.

( ) 41. be absolutely consistent in the enforcement of rules; treat all offenders alike.

( ) 42. discuss quiet hour rules with groups of girls to bring about better enforcement.

( ) 43. get the cooperation of the girls in the maintenance of certain standards of dress and behavior in the public rooms of the college and on the street.

( ) 44. encourage the girls to organize after-dinner discussions on topics of current interest.

( ) 45. provide opportunities to meet interesting people from outside the college.

( ) 46. encourage the girl to make the most of the cultural resources of the community by her own enthusiastic acquaintance with them.

( ) 47. confer with the girls regarding dormitory plans and work out plans cooperatively with them.

( ) 48. encourage the girls to work in community and civic enterprises where their programs permit.

( ) 49. refer those with complicated problems to persons who can give them more expert help.

( ) 50. see that the public rooms of the college are as attractive and comfortable as available funds can make them.

Appendix B

QUESTIONNAIRE FOR HEADS
OF RESIDENCE

COLLEGES AND UNIVERSITIES REPLYING
TO THE QUESTIONNAIRE

Boston University
College of New Rochelle
Hiram College
Indiana University
Lake Erie College
Louisiana State College
Ohio Wesleyan University
Pembroke College
Pomona College
Sophie Newcomb College

Stanford University
State University of Iowa
Stephens College
University of Mississippi
University of New Hampshire
University of New Mexico
University of Vermont
University of Wisconsin
Vassar College
Wellesley College

QUESTIONNAIRE

NUMBER OF STUDENTS IN RESIDENCE..........COLLEGE......................
AVERAGE NUMBER IN EACH HALL..............DATE......................

1. Think of a girl in the dormitory who came to you recently. Write as accurately as possible what was said by both of you in the interview or series of interviews. What were some of the results of the counseling?

2. *a.* On whom may you yourself call for expert help in your counseling or assisting of the girls?

b. To what officer or individual may you refer the girls?

3. What do girls come to talk to you about? Arrange these opportunities for counseling approximately in order of frequency, with the most common first.

4. When you first began to work with dormitory students, which of these understandings and skills did you find you most needed in your personal relations and counseling with them? Please check to the left several and/ or add others below which you feel are important.

[Note: These thirty-one items (for example, "knowledge of occupations and of opportunities in different fields" and "ability to formulate questions skillfully, following leads of students") are omitted because this question did not yield usable data.]